Reflections Inspired by Lilias Trotter

IMAGES *of*
FAITH

MIRIAM HUFFMAN ROCKNESS

DEVOTIONAL EDITION | VOLUMES 1 & 2

OXVISION
BOOKS

ISBN: 978 1 938068 32 4

Library of Congress Control Number: 2019931796

Published by Oxvision Books
4001 Tamiami Trail North, Suite 250, Naples, FL 34103
Find us at: oxvisionmedia.com   oxvisionfilms.com

Images of Faith is published in partnership with the Lilias Trotter Legacy Group
Find us at: liliastrotter.com

DEDICATION

Alasdair McLaren, whose tireless collaboration has been invaluable from the beginning and throughout my search for Lilias.

His partnership has been essential in resurrecting her story.

and

Brian & Sally Oxley, whose vision and generosity have made it possible to reintroduce the life and art of Lilias Trotter to a new generation.

A bee comforted me very much this morning concerning the

desultoriness that troubles me in our work . . . He was hovering

among some blackberry sprays, just touching the flowers here

and there in a very tentative way, yet all unconsciously,

life—life—life was left behind at every touch, as the miracle-

working pollen grains were transferred to the place where

they could set the unseen spring working. We have only to see

to it that we are surcharged, like the bees, with potential life.

It is God and His eternity that will do the work. Yet He needs

His wandering, desultory bees!

—Lilias Trotter, Diary July 9, 1907

CONTENTS

FOREWORD

Images of Faith: Reflections Inspired by Lilias Trotter is the rare volume that illustrates some of the significant ways that spiritual truth may impact our daily realities. Indeed, all of these reflections are taken from the ordinary moments of life; because of this, they are easily accessible to us. Miriam H. Rockness, who serves as guide to these offerings, has been reading and pondering the words of the Anglican artist and missionary Lilias Trotter for three decades. In *Images of Faith*, we reap the benefit of Miriam's dedicated investment of time as we, too, are invited to consider the deep meaning of Lilias's life, and not just the biographical facts.

In *Letters to Malcolm*, C. S. Lewis's most comprehensive statement on the Christian discipline of prayer, he writes: "We may ignore, but we can nowhere evade, the presence of God. The world is crowded with Him. He walks everywhere *incognito*. And the *incognito* is not always hard to penetrate. The real labour is to remember, to attend. In fact, to come awake. Still more, to remain awake."

Lilias Trotter understood this truth well, and she spent a lifetime using her artistic gifts to reveal the presence of God that she found everywhere . . . gloriously made known in the beauty of creation as well as in the lives of the people around her. In *Images of Faith*, Miriam Rockness invites us to learn this art of seeing, so that we are able, as C. S. Lewis declared, "to attend . . . to come awake . . . still more, to remain awake" to the reality of God's presence in our own lives. This is an invitation well worth accepting.

—Marjorie Lamp Mead
Editor of *VII* and Associate Director
The Marion E. Wade Center
Wheaton College, Illinois

INTRODUCTION

Images of Faith: Reflections Inspired by Lilias Trotter is an inside view of
Lilias Trotter's personal pilgrimage, culled from her diaries, journals, and published

works, written and painted over the forty years of her life in
Algeria. It is also my pilgrimage of faith as I reflect on those
writings and watercolors.

I first became acquainted with Lilias Trotter through out-
of-print books, by and about her, in the late 1980s. I was a busy
pastor's wife and mother of three children. What could a single
woman (no children) from a wealthy West End London family, who lived among
the poor of Algeria more than one hundred years ago, possibly say to me? What
did an artist whose raw talent captured the attention of John Ruskin have to say to
me, struggling to capture a little beauty in my corner of the world?

As it turned out, a great deal! Her insights based on eternal verities of
Scripture and tempered with hard-won life experience cut through current trends
of thought to the very essence of my soul. It had the ring of truth, and I simply
couldn't get enough of her practical perspective. She wrote of discouragement,
struggle, perseverance, joy, love, prayer, the paradoxes of size and significance, of
power and weakness—from God's point of view—and, well, just about every topic
that mattered to me. She illuminated many of these eloquently worded truths with
exquisite watercolors. Lessons from God's Word and God's world—an inward and
outward vision—became clear through parables from nature.

She became a mentor to me, fleshing out truth in the arena of day-to-day
living. I wanted to know more about her and find everything written or painted
by her. I wanted to share my discovery with others. Thus began a quest that led
eventually to my writing her biography (*Passion for the Impossible: The Life of Lilias
Trotter*, 1999) and compiling some of her writings and watercolors (*Blossom in the
Desert: Reflections of Faith in the Art and Writings of Lilias Trotter*, 2007)—a journey
that is documented, in part, in the film of her life, *Many Beautiful Things* (2015).

Fast forward several years. Our children are grown and raising families of their own in three different states, my husband is retired, we have moved to a small town in central Florida. Once again I turn to Lilias, as I process challenges (and joys) of transition and adjustment in this new chapter of my life. I determined to indulge myself in writing reflections on the writings and watercolors that have special resonance for me now—and in seasons past. And, once again, I find that Lily's lessons still hold.

The duty of a biographer is to present an objective account of the subject's life—to paint a realistic portrait—faithful to the facts. I now have the luxury of approaching the themes and topics of her life from a purely subjective point of view: what they mean to me on my journey—present and past. My selection of these topics is purely personal: words and art that have spoken deeply to me and guided me on my pilgrimage of faith.

Lilias wrote two comprehensive treatises on the Christian life: *Parables of the Cross* (an English devotional) and *The Sevenfold Secret* (for the Arab Sufi mystics). She considered these two books to be her most important works, with a definitive purpose and focus.

Images of Faith, in contrast, is an inside view of her spiritual formation, her process of integrating scriptural precepts with life experience. It is a close-up and personal glimpse of Lilias Trotter's pilgrimage of faith: an adult lifetime of daily learning until the very end of her time on earth. It is also my pilgrimage: how she has guided me through almost three decades of life. My selections were initially determined not by set topics or chronology but by my own journey and how she spoke to my spirit. These selections fell roughly into eight major topics: joy, God, redemption, spiritual growth, prayer, service, refreshment, and faith. While these categories don't comprise a comprehensive statement of her spirituality, they are representative of the themes that guided her life. In 2017 about half of these *Images of Faith* reflections were published as volume 1, in a beautiful art-gift book (Oxvision). Now readers have volumes 1 & 2 bound together in an illustrated devotional edition.

So I share my reflections because I believe they hold universal truths relevant to all pilgrims, regardless of where they are on the journey. I invite the reader to examine with me the "images of faith" culled from her legacy—written and visual.

Our Works Will Follow Us

Our works will follow us. God may use, by reason of the wonderful solidarity of His Church, the things that He has wrought in us, for the blessing of souls unknown to us: as these twigs and leaves of bygone years, whose individuality is forgotten, pass on vitality still to the newborn wood-sorrel. God only knows the endless possibilities that lie folded in each one of us! —Parables of the Cross

Their works do follow them.

. . . for their deeds will follow them.   —Revelation 14:13

At first glance, the above painting appears to be but dead twigs and leaves. Then one notes a sap green sprig of *"new-born wood sorrel"* above which are printed words from the book of Revelation: "Their works do follow them." Lilias concludes her book *Parables of the Cross* with words that were both prescient for her and potentially for all who follow Christ: *"The results need not end with our earthly days. Should Jesus tarry our works will follow us . . ."*

Even as Lilias developed these thoughts, inspired by both God's Word and works, she was no doubt integrating them with her own life experience: difficult conditions, little apparent results. Her intended break, the summer of 1895, extended into the autumn then winter months including "bed rest" doctor's orders. Weakness and sleeplessness reflected the strains of ministry, yet permitted the prolonged period of rest during which she penned her devotional classic.

The belief, based on Scripture, that what one sows for eternity continues beyond one's earthly span motivated and sustained her as she scattered seeds over the face of Algeria for decades. She saw lives touched by the *"light and life and love of God"* and ministries developed that furthered and deepened that vision. When she died in 1928, thirty members of the Algiers Mission Band continued to minister through fifteen stations and outposts along the coast of North Africa and into the Southlands, later merging with what is now Arab World Ministry of Pioneers. There are reports in present-day Algeria of God's Spirit working across the land, even indications of a fledgling church. She left a written legacy of English devotional books, most notably the *Parables of the Cross* and *Parables of the Christ-life* plus her consummate masterpiece for the Sufi mystics, *The Sevenfold Secret.*

I have no reason to believe that as she recorded the daily events of her life in the small page-a-day leather-bound diaries, she would have imagined that her personal legacy—her life defined in words and watercolors—would be revived a century later. Yet this is what is happening even as I write. God is using *"twigs and leaves of bygone years"* for His purposes: *"the blessing of souls unknown to us."*

Things have been happening quietly over the past three or four decades converging in a story of how, through the *"wonderful solidarity of His Church,"* God continues to use her life and legacy. More than thirty years ago, a devoted English missionary remained in Algeria, at the onset of political turmoil, to close down the work and pack up the archives (including Lilias's diaries and journals) to ship to safety, ultimately in England. Not long after, on another continent, two American sisters gave their library of Trotter books to a (then) young minister's wife and mother of three children. Her passion for the books and a hunger to learn more about their author and subjects led her, eventually, to the archives in England and to the publishing of a biography of Lilias Trotter, *A Passion for the Impossible*, plus *A Blossom in the Desert*, a compilation of her writings and paintings long hidden in relative obscurity in three cardboard boxes!

Fast forward to 2014. A couple "discovered" Lilias through these books, and they envisioned a film short to introduce her to the people of Japan, believing her art would appeal to their artistic sensibility, and their hearts. This led to our meeting—a union that sparked other exciting discoveries, journals and sketchbooks, copies of the "missing" Ruskin letters to Lilias—expanding the original concept into an hour-long documentary, *Many Beautiful Things*, which premiered internationally and in the USA at the Manchester and Heartland film festivals, respectively, the summer and fall of 2015 and was launched nationwide at the National Gallery of Art, February 2016.

Many Beautiful Things presents the people and land of Lilias's beloved North Africa through her exquisite art, using techniques and equipment unimagined during her lifetime. It is the story of this remarkable woman who made a life-altering decision about the role of art in her life—and how God used both her art and her life for purposes being realized even now after all these years. But above all, it is the story of God and how He continues to work His purposes still unknown to us in His time and His way. Only God knows the endless possibilities that lie in her life and legacy.

And(!) *"God only knows the endless possibilities that lie folded in each of us!"* We have no idea how God will use those things we do and say, great or small, for His purposes. We do know that what is sown for eternal purposes will *"pass on vitality"* after our own *"individuality is forgotten."* And that is what counts: to be faithful to our understanding of His plan for us.

I conclude with Lilias's final challenge in the *Parables of the Cross*: *"Shall we not let Him have His way? Shall we not go all lengths with Him in His plans for us—not, as these 'green things upon the earth' in their unconsciousness but with the glory of free choice? Shall we not translate the story of their little lives into our own?"*

God only knows the endless possibilities that lie folded in each of us!

Lord, thank You for the spiritual legacy of Lilias Trotter.
Help me to discover the possibilities You have enfolded within me.

Part 1

Images of Joy

Beholdings!

. . . going day by day for what the Japanese would call "beholdings"
& bring(ing) back vivid word-pictures of the same that are a joy . . .
They went with the intent of shewing Margaret [sister] a row of
wonderful cypresses, silhouetted against the curve of the bay, with the port
lying below, the tracery of breakwaters & shipping basins shewing prune
coloured on the opal sea.   —Diary October 1925

Painting: from *Between the Desert & the Sea*

For since the creation of the world God's invisible qualities—his eternal
power and divine nature—have been clearly seen, being understood from
what has been made, so that men are without excuse.   —Romans 1:20

BEHOLDINGS! Lilias, in the above diary entry, was content to enjoy word-pictures
of "beholdings" that her sister brought from her excursions to her bedside, she
being too weak to venture beyond the four walls of her room. And, from the
window of that same room, Lilias observed "beholdings" that gladdened her heart:
"*Lovelier than ever, this year, has seemed the interweaving of autumn & spring, till you
can hardly tell which it is—the tiny stars of white jonquils into the withered grass—&
the golden crocus among the falling leaves, & the amethyst Judas blossom, not knowing
what to do with itself, from the wealth of sap that the first rains have brought rising.*"
Lilias brought to her final years a practice of a lifetime or, in the words of

Flannery O'Connor, "a habit of being." From her earliest years, she recorded what she saw in little pocket sketchbooks, capturing a host of "beholdings"—a skill that John Ruskin noted in his "The Art of England" lecture to be "what we should all like to be able to do . . ." All the while she was training her eyes to see: a "habit" that brought joy even to her most difficult days.

I write at my kitchen table. A photograph, a handful of shells, and a heartful of memories—beholdings!—are what remain of a family vacation, twenty-one people strong, at a Florida beach house. I try to capture images in my journal, sounds and sights: waves pounding the shore; sea birds swooping down for their evening catch; sea grapes flanking the boardwalk leading to the beach; laughter (and wails) of children; these same children nut-brown from the sun, seated around a large wooden table, appetites teased from fresh air and salt water; adults gathered, after the children are bedded, talking late into the night.

What I do by intent—collect beholdings to record and remember—our young grandchildren do by instinct, still awed by everyday wonders. From the porch rocking chair overlooking the beach, I was eyewitness of wonder and firsthand recipient of children's beholdings. They came to me—a convenient anchor—to proffer their treasures: sea glass, an odd configuration of moss, a crab shield, shells of all shapes and sizes. Breathless with excitement, they announced the miracle of hatching sea turtles making their tenuous maiden voyage out to sea.

What occurs on a vacation or scenic trip can be, should be, cultivated on a daily basis. Call it "grace" or "blessings" or "gifts"—or, as did Lilias, "beholdings"—it is less about the name than the reality. Beauty is within our reach regardless of our immediate circumstance. It exists in the simplicity of ordinary rites and routines. I believe that beauty is one of God's loveliest ways of reminding us that He is . . . and that He cares . . . Pointers, in a sense, to heaven. And, in turn, I'm convinced, that being attuned to beauty is no small thing—whether in the grandeur of a mountain range or the minutia of a cobweb, the nuzzle of a beloved pet or, in the words of Sara Teasdale, "children's faces looking up holding wonder like a cup . . ."

Sometimes beauty surprises us. Serendipity. Sometimes it seduces us, as did the glimpses of joy that C. S. Lewis, as a child, saw in Beatrix Potter's illustration of Autumn, intimating to him "something other." Beauty sustains us during times of unrelenting duress: for example, the renewal of spring during a seemingly endless war, evidenced by green shoots and yellow daffodils breaking through cracks in barricades of sandbags—described by V. Sackville-West in her *Country Notes in Wartime*. And sometimes it *saves* us: Viktor Frankl's glimpse of "the mountains of Salzburg with their summits glowing in the sunset, through the little barred windows of a prison carriage . . ."; fragments from a Beethoven concerto, piercing the darkness of a concentration camp barrack, heard by Elie Wiesel; a pot of tulips in a hospital room . . .

Whether by surprise or design, I am continually startled by "beholdings." If I could, I would paint them, like Lilias, but instead I record them in words, a literary depiction in my journal. "Beholding" I write in bold print; then I jot it down, one at a time, as it happens: scent of orange blossoms . . . a single orchid bloom, survivor of a neglected plant . . . a trio of butterflies dancing above lantana . . . a peacock reclining alongside a back country road . . . a clean child wrapped in terry cloth, wet hair slicked behind ears . . . a letter in the mailbox . . . recorded music filling the house . . . a cat sunning in a patch of sunlight . . .

St. Augustine said: "The soul is weighed in the balance by what delights her. Delight or enjoyment sets the soul in her ordered place." Little matter if we translate that delight in paint or print, in music or in spoken word. What matters is that we do behold. And *wonder*!

⊱ ⊱ ⊱

God, the world is full of Your glory! May the beholdings
I witness today point me to You, the Creator.

Sunshine of My Happy Heart

The peaks of the Mischabel were just shouting for joy this morning in radiant snow, after a day's storm, and the late filaments of cloud were dancing round their crests. Oh it is a wonderful world. —Diary August 28, 1901

Painting: from Travel Journal 1896, 1897

The heavens declare the glory of God;
  the skies proclaim the work of his hands. —Psalm 19:1

Autumn chased us southward, tinting leaves with traces of color—just as we were leaving. Illinois . . . Indiana . . . Ohio . . . West Virginia . . . Indian summer it was for us Floridians, just missing the long-awaited cool of a new season.

Until today. Autumn has finally caught up with us—in Florida! Temperatures fell during the night, and this morning I walked out to a cool fall day. A flash of color caught my eye. I reached down and lifted autumn into my hand: a single leaf aflame with crimson tinged in gold. A cardinal, bright as the leaf, darted above my path: autumn on the wing!

Oh, it *is* a wonderful world! Whether the snowcapped mountain Lilias recorded in words and watercolors or the color-washed Florida leaf resting in my hand—all stands still in one's heart brimming with the beauty. I want to freeze the moment—the autumn-ness of it—capture it in a photo or painting or poem. But I know that my best efforts would fall short of the reality. Such moments can't be captured as much as simply remembered. Remembered for the jolt of joy, the momentary transcendence from common cares and exertions that mark one's ordinary days.

Capture an elusive heart-catching moment? No. But cultivate? Yes. Cultivating an awareness of all that is best, is what we not only were created but instructed to do. The apostle Paul echoed the psalmist in urging an awareness of "whatever is true, whatever is noble, whatever is right, whatever is pure, whatever is lovely, whatever is admirable—" adding, "if anything is excellent or praiseworthy—think about such things" (Philippians 4:8).

Consider the pages of my well-worn red leather journals. So quick am I to take to pen to hack out my problems, to process my pain. So stingy with my joy, the pull of gravity favoring the negative. Yet both exist, side by side.

I must learn to live fully my joy in the moment. And train myself to record the positive beholdings of the heart alongside the beholdings of my eye. It is a choice, really, a matter of focus as there is much, indeed, to weigh down one's spirit. But there is so much to elevate one's soul as well. John Ruskin once observed about a gutter: "If you look deep enough, you may see the serious blue of far-off sky and the passing pure clouds. It is at your will what you see in that despised stream, either the refuse of the street or the image of the sky."

"It is at our will," what we choose to see, upon what we choose to focus. Easy, one might say, for Lilias to exult in the dancing clouds and radiant snow of Switzerland. But she brought the same eyes to a North African landscape that many considered parched, dull, even hostile. Her lifelong friend, Constance Padwick, noted: "For her, God's world in every aspect was supremely worth the watching. His ways in nature were her poetry. His ways with humankind were her romance." At the end of her life, Lilias marveled, "*Oh how good it is that I have been sent here to such beauty!*"

It is up to my "will" what I choose to consume me. I can be bogged down with the weight of unfinished work . . . hurting or hurtful people . . . worries or concerns about the future . . . Or I can be elevated by the wonders of this world—the leaf on the ground, the bird on the wing . . . the unmerited love of grandchildren . . . friendships nourished by e-mail or phone, a meal or a visit . . . a loving God revealed through outward vision and inward quickenings . . .

Pain and suffering will always be present in this broken world. At least for now. But so will the beauty and the wonder. Which do I choose to see when I gaze into the pooled water: "the refuse of the street or the image of the sky"? Which do *you* choose?

❧ ❧ ❧

Sunshine of my happy heart.
God, of my praise, to Thee be praise.

—Amy Carmichael

The Speech of Angels

We are lodged in rooms off the Central Hall [at Miechovitz in northern Germany]*—& before it is daylight the chorales begin there softly like birds singing in the dawn . . . and all day long there is a ripple of gladness.*

—Diary November 14, 1908

Painting: from *The Voice of the Bird among the Flowers* (a picture book for children)

I will sing and make music to the LORD.   —Psalm 27:6

LILIAS ENDED AN INTENSIVE two-month speaking schedule in Scandinavia, in the autumn of 1908, with an unexpected trip to Germany. Encouraged by Baroness Kurcks of Sweden, Lilias consented to a meeting with Sister Eva of Friedenshort. This was the beginning of a lifelong friendship and the continuing source of inspiration for both of these women with similar affluent backgrounds.

Miechovitz was in a mining district on the spur of the Carpathians, buffeted by the bitter winds of Russia. And yet, as Lilias observed, *"Inwardly it was all aglow, as I never knew a place to be in all my life—on fire with a spirit of sacrifice that did not even know itself to be sacrifice, it is so the natural expression of love."*

It had been a small mission outpost until the time of the Welsh Revival when Sister Eva's lifelong search for God was met *"by a full drought from His fountain."* The mission grew from a staff of 24 to 150 "sisters," the household numbering 300, including orphans, students, infirmed villagers, babies—to say nothing of other related ministries.

It was the music from the orphan children—*"like birds singing in the dawn"*—that awakened Lilias every morning and set the course of gladness for the rest of the day. What an inspired ending to the rigors of a speaking ministry and renewal for the relaunch of ministry in Algiers.

Music. "Music is well said to be the speech of angels," wrote Thomas Carlyle, "in fact, nothing among the utterances allowed to man is felt to be so divine." How does one explain the mystery of matching pitch with rhythm, to make a pleasing melody? Or pairing pitches to that tune—adding, perhaps, percussion or horn or strings—resulting in glorious harmonies? How is it that the experiencing of music transcends the physical sense of hearing or the neurological complexities of the brain, penetrating to the deepest places of the soul?

Little matter the simplicity or complexity: a single line of monastic chant . . . a simple hymn tune chorded with four notes and linked with text . . . a haunting folk song accompanied with a six-string acoustic guitar . . . the plaintive melodies of American spirituals . . . wordless music—a sonata, a symphony. Or put it all together—stage, actors, song, libretto, orchestra—into complex operatic form. "The twelve notes in each octave and the varieties of rhythm offer opportunities that all of human genius will never exhaust," noted Igor Stravinsky.

Many people, like myself, can trace key moments in life through particular songs or music associated with those events. Music captures the emotional essence of an experience that can only, with difficulty, be put into words.

Three such incidents immediately come to mind: two were in Israel although separated by many years; one was in a boat, on the Sea of Galilee. My husband and I were "alone" together, separated from family and friends, the overcast skies and choppy water matching my mood. Then from another section of the boat, a group of travelers launched into song: the words of a beloved old hymn, "Dear Lord and Father of Mankind," to an unfamiliar but compelling tune. The clear voices in lilting English accent wrapped the threads of sound around my heart, uniting the Church Universal, here in Israel, in their England, and in my own USA:

> Drop Thy still dews of quietness till all our strivings cease;
> Take from our souls the strain and stress,
> And let our ordered lives confess the beauty of Thy peace.

The second "Israel Experience" was in the Jewish Quarter of the Old City. I heard the heartrending music of a string quartet before I saw them: four gentlemen seated on folding chairs, in an open space within the cloistered walkway—instrument cases open to receive the chance token of appreciation. They had been members, I learned, of a famed Russian orchestra, now refugees piecing together a living—their price for freedom.

Most recently music connected me across the miles, via phone, with my mother who was finding less to talk about as her world became smaller. And yet! She would come alive when I would recall a beloved song—some from her early camp meeting years—and together we would sing those texts of affirmation, she filling in where I would forget the words. "Leaning on the Everlasting Arms." "Great Is Thy Faithfulness." "Come, Ye Disconsolate."

Music touches places in the heart when words alone fail. It comforts and consoles. Music expresses thoughts unutterable. "Music is the shorthand of emotions," Tolstoy proclaimed, conveying emotion for which words are inadequate. "Music," according to Dietrich Bonhoeffer, "will help dissolve your perplexities and purify your character and sensibilities and in time of care and sorrow will keep a function of joy alive in you."

I clean house to the lyrical music of Mozart and worship to the hymn lines of Isaac Watts and Charles Wesley. Soulful tunes—folk songs and spirituals and gospel music and Vaughn Williams's arrangements—fill my heart. A catchy foot-tapping tune from a popular score or praise chorus invariably lifts my spirits. And from time to time I devote an entire evening to a concert beautifully staged and orchestrated with perfect acoustics. Still the sweet song of a child (grandchild!) catches me unexpectedly with a jolt of joy!

Music! Who but God could have imagined such a gift?! The language of angels; the transport of mortals to the infinite.

God, You have filled Your world with birdsong, rushing wind, and the splashing of rain. You have gifted humankind with the skill to create sounds and songs. Speak to my soul through music and lift my heart in praise to You.

February Flowers

The spring flowers that stand all about my room in Arab pots of green and yellow earthenware bring a very real revelation of Him, "by whom were all things created." The clear happiness of the daisies and the radiant shout of the celandines, and the deep sweet joy of the great almond blossoms with their mystical hearts—all are literal foreshadowing of the "gladness above His fellows."

—Diary February 13, 1927

Painting: from Between the Desert & the Sea

> Great are the works of the LORD;
>   they are pondered by all who delight in them.   —Psalm 111:2

SPRING ARRIVES EARLY IN CENTRAL FLORIDA. Sap pushing dead leaves from trees; buds swelling from branches, orange blossoms scenting the air. Indications of new life abound: bud and leaf and frond.

Nothing is so beautiful as Spring—
when weeds, in wheels, shoot long and lovely and lush;
. . .
What is all this juice and all this joy?
I strain of the earth's sweet being in the beginning.
—Gerard Manley Hopkins

Even as I savor each indication of new life—spring!—flower shops
and grocery shelves are flooded with bulb flowers evoking for me the
quiddity of my childhood. Spring flowers: narcissus, tulip, daffodil, crocus.
A northern spring!

February flowers. Native beauty; northern nostalgia. Garden or green
house. Little matter. Each speaks its special message through shape and
texture and hue. Straight through the senses to the heart.

God spoke to Lilias through His Handiwork. Flowers were, for her,
His intimate love letter. Each stage of growth, from bud to bloom to seed,
was not only a source of delight but a message straight from God—*a
very real revelation of Him 'by whom were all things created.'"* Daisy . . . cyclamen
. . . poppy . . . soldanella . . . dandelion . . . desert crocus . . . Each contained a
special lesson. Each pointed to its Creator.

Lilias's early pocket sketchbooks captured, in watercolors, English
wayside flowers and alpine wildflowers. Her first year in Algeria she
painted flowers unique to North Africa along with vignettes of people
and places, and later she recorded desert flowers of an even more exotic
character. During her pilgrimage to Palestine, she observed: *". . . Galilee—all
in its spring beauty of flowers & budding fig-trees—all our own North African
flowers . . . & it brings a hallowing over our blossom time there to know that they
have their sister flowers here & that they must have been dear to the Lord's
eyes & heart"* (March 26, 1924).

While confined to bed, during her final years, she culled images of flora
and fauna from forty years of loving—village, plain, desert—and locked them
into the delicate paintings (along with the people and places) that became

the treasured publication *Between the Desert & the Sea*, her love affair with North Africa.

Lilias's classic work *Parables of the Cross* demonstrates through the life stages of plants and flowers how death is necessary for life to continue in the physical world—and in the spiritual:

> *"Death is the gate of life." Does it look so to us? Have we learnt to go down, once and again, into its gathering shadows in quietness and confidence, knowing that there is always "a better resurrection" beyond?*
>
> *It is in the stages of a plant's growth, its budding and blossoming and seed-bearing, that this lesson has come to me: the lesson of death in its delivering power. It has come as no mere far-fetched image, but as one of the many voices in which God speaks, bringing strength and gladness from His Holy Place.*

Flowers "speak" their own individual story: poppy ... buttercup ... dandelion ... vetch. Like the *Parables of the Cross*, they speak of living, yes, but of dying as well. Dying in order to live, *"bringing strength and gladness from His Holy Place."*

> *Thank You, God, for the ever-changing beauty of Your natural world.*
> *Speak to me through Your handiwork and renew me with Your fresh returns.*

Bound and Yet Unbound

*The milky looking glacier spoke with God's voice this morning—so obedient to
its course in its narrow bed,—yet just—tossing with freedom & swing in every
motion—such a picture of the rivers "of living water"—bound & yet unbound.*

—Journal August 8, 1899

Painting: from Travel Journal 1899

But the man who looks intently into the perfect law that gives
freedom, and continues to do this, not forgetting what he has heard,
but doing it—he will be blessed in what he does.   —James 1:25

I LOVE IT WHEN LILIAS MINISTERS TO ME—through other people. Such
was my experience this week when I read a devotional that included a quote
from Lilias. I looked up the quotation, in context, and discovered a painting
of the same.

Subject? Obedience. A word most often associated with "rules"—one
short (negative) step from restrictions. And yet, Lilias chose to illustrate

"obedience" with a glacier *"tossing with freedom & swing in every motion."*
Is that true? Is there, in fact, evidence (if not proof) of liberty within limits . . . freedom within boundaries . . . ? Or, as Lilias stated, the paradox of being *"bound & yet unbound"*?

I look to my heroes of faith and find C. S. Lewis on my short list. Lewis was a man of faith with a lifestyle light years from mine: scholar (Oxford and Cambridge-based academician), single for most of his adult years, and British. Convicted of his need for a spiritual director, Lewis chose to place himself in a relationship of accountability—a decision challenged by his own innate "private" nature. His choice, Anglican priest Walter Adams, would have perhaps the most profound input on Lewis's development during his spiritually formative years.

Adams seldom missed an opportunity to remind people to "look after the roots and the fruits will look after themselves." Adams and Lewis agreed that the "deep watering of the roots required radical obedience to every thing the Lord required, regardless of how small or mundane it seemed." Lewis wrote: "Discipline is the key to all doors" (*Seeking the Secret Place: The Spiritual Formation of C. S. Lewis*, by Lyle Dorsett).

Letter writing was one such thing Lewis believed God required of him. If readers took the trouble to write to him, it was his inviolable obligation to respond to them whether to answer questions or respond to their gratitude. Little did he realize when he submitted to that discipline how, a decade later, he would be bombarded with mail, his writings and radio lectures having made him a household name. When questioned about this "bane of my life," he never veered from his original belief, "When Christ gives an order it must be done," even if he didn't fully understand why. While he understood the immediate value of any writing that "illuminated the heart," he didn't know what would become of these letters (many now in published "collections"): a spiritual legacy for generations to come.

The common perception is that "obedience" to some higher power or rule stifles freedom. Yet Lewis insisted: "Obedience is the road to freedom" (*Letters to Malcolm*). Life confirms the same. Consider the value of boundaries in art.

Take the sonnet, for example, a poetic form with a fixed pattern of lines, meter, and rhyme. From this exacting structure has emerged some of the world's greatest poetry: Shakespeare's penetrating insight into human nature; Milton's profound resolution to his blindness; Elizabeth Barrett Browning's outpouring of passion and love. Thought compressed to crystalline hardness radiates with the clarity and brilliance of a diamond. The precision and power that makes these sonnets so compelling must be attributed, in part, to the defining and refining role of restriction. One could go on and on with like illustrations in various disciplines: sports, science, music, for a start.

Back to point. These are only examples, in microcosm, of what God intended for us—lives rich and free and joy filled—when we live within His prescribed boundaries. He has given us a rulebook (Scripture) and a Guide (the Holy Spirit) to instruct us and inspire us.

Frankly, I really don't like to be told what to do. But what if I'm instructed by someone I really trust? What if it is for my good? My *highest* good? The obedience of which Lewis and Lilias wrote was, of course, to the God of the Bible. Can He be trusted? Does He have my highest good in mind? If so . . . surely I must "trust and obey," as summed in the old gospel song, "for there's no other way to be happy in Jesus . . ."

Like the glacier "*so obedient to its course in its narrow bed—such a picture of the rivers 'of living water'—bound & yet unbound!*"

Strengthen me, Lord, to embrace the obedience that leads to true freedom.
May I experience the joy of living this day within the boundaries of Your will.

The Gladness of My Joy

We speak of the God of Love and the God of Peace—so seldom of the God of Joy. God is the God of joy, and we must drink in the spirit of His joy. And flowers speak of the gladness that is in the heart of God. Flowers are not a necessity—they are just an overflowing of God's gladness and if we look closely at each, it seems to reveal His joy each in a different way. "Thy Face the heart of every flower that blows." You can read Him in them . . . God the gladness of my joy . . . the merry heart of the celandines and the pure simple happiness of the primrose and the shout of the daffodils' golden trumpet. He didn't promise us ease and comfort—but He did promise joy which we may have in the midst of any weight or heaviness that may be ours to bear.

—Notes from Lilias's study on the temple carvings July 17, 1928

Painting: from Diary 1899

Therefore God, your God, has set you above your companions
by anointing you with the oil of joy.   —Psalm 45:7

THESE WORDS ABOUT JOY were penciled faintly in Lilias's final entry of her journal: July 17, 1928. They were notes for Sunday afternoon Bible readings, based on the carvings on Solomon's temple, during the lull of the summer when most of the workers took their much-needed breaks. The remaining few gathered around her bed for what would be her last meditations on earth. The next month, on August 27, she would be "Home" for *her* well-deserved rest.

Joy was a common theme woven throughout the pages of her diaries and her life. Friends testified to the same, quoting Lilias: "Oh, we do need a real laugh sometimes, don't we?" And, "I wish so-and-so could laugh more," she said of a new worker, "but she'll shake free. They always do."

Clearly, she experienced daily all manner of concerns that fairly could be called "joy killers." Who can't relate to that? If only, we think . . . if only this person, this illness, this financial pinch, this situation could be altered—then I could be happy.

But the joy Lilias described was not determined by outward events or circumstances. It was the joy Jesus mentioned on His way to Calvary, promising His disciples "a full measure" of His joy and echoing the psalmist's declaration, "Your God has set you above your companions by anointing you with the oil of joy" (Psalm 45:7).

Joy stands in sharp contrast to happiness, which tends to be directly related to our circumstance: Christmas Day surrounded by family; a long-desired trip; acquisition of a longed-for house or car or object; a good medical report. Joy holds firm when all the above fails or falls away.

The joy of which Lilias spoke continues even when "happiness" fades, when the externals that buoyed our spirits no longer hold. This kind of joy runs deeper than all external prompts or perks. It is based on the deep and confident assurance of God's love and work in our lives. That *He* will be present no matter what! "*He didn't promise us ease and comfort—but He did promise joy which we may have in the midst of any weight or heaviness that may be ours to bear.*"

I trust you can think of someone who embodies that kind of joy—in Scripture (Paul!) and in your own personal network. I was privileged to have that modeled by my mother. She was not, by nature, a bouncy positive person. Her temperament was contemplative, even melancholic. What's more, I witnessed, through the years, her experiencing her own share of setbacks and discouragements.

And yet, in the very midst of personal and maternal battles, she chose to focus on the small joys amidst the big trials; she chose to see redeeming elements in troublesome days. She used occasions of doubt to remind us (and herself) of God's past faithfulness. During a given struggle, she celebrated life, often turning to her tea-tray set with a Lusterware pot, bone china plates and cups, silver spoons and tea strainer, and (when in season) a flower in a cut-glass vase, inviting us into the comfort of this ceremony. Her legacy, in part, was her example of "living above the circumstance."

I have all of the above now—her tools of trade—and I also have the "inside story" in her journals: records of hard days as well as glorious. It all rings true: even as she records with heartbreaking accuracy the struggles of her everyday life, she rejoices in all manner of beauty that surrounds her—nature, family, and, yes, tea time—and gives witness to her confidence that God will not forsake her or hers.

So, I move forward, secure in the confidence that my emotional barometer need not be determined by circumstances, which change like the weather, but in an unchanging God—who is the gladness of my joy!

❧ ❧ ❧

God, let me sense the gladness of Your joy that transcends the circumstances of this day.

Glad in the Present Day

You are right to be glad in His April days while He gives them. Every stage of the heavenly growth in us is lovely to Him. He is the God of the daisies and the lambs and the merry child hearts! It may be that no such path of loss lies before

Painting: from Diary 1906

you; there are people like the lands where spring and summer weave the year between them, and the autumn processes are hardly noticed as they come and go. The one thing is to keep obedient in spirit, then you will be ready to let the flower-time pass if He bids you, when the sun of His love has worked some more ripening. You will feel by then that to try to keep the withering blossoms would be to cramp and ruin your soul. It is loss to keep when God says "give."

—*Parables of the Cross*

This is the day the Lord has made;
let us rejoice and be glad in it.

—Psalm 118:24

Such a beautiful autumn day! I sit on a rocking chair and savor the view from our front porch: blooms of purple, red, magenta, pink—bush and border, arbor and window box—a kaleidoscope of color. Butterflies flutter above lantana lured by their blossoms of yellow and orange. White billowy clouds scuttle across a china-blue sky. A bright red cardinal darts from tree to fence to tree. The air is alive with bird song and the peck, peck, pecking of—a woodpecker! My heart fairly bursts with the joy of it all. October in Florida.

And my heart fills with gratitude for the dear clapboard cottage that shelters us, fitted with furnishings from our past homes, augmented now with treasured objects from parents and grandparents. Photographs and paintings and pictures mix with objects of sentiment—artifacts of family and friends. Just "things," yes, but things rich with heritage and memories—bridges connecting us to people and places ever dear to us.

I ask: do these things mean too much to me? Is it "right" to care so much for what, at best, is transient? I remember asking that same question several decades ago. We had just moved in to an old manse newly refurbished by the church. I would walk through the large rooms with high ceilings, hardwood floors, walls and trim freshly painted in *my* colors. I would savor my view of pond and park and live oak trees—and wonder: Is it right to love it so completely? It didn't help that at that very time I was working my way through Dietrich Bonhoeffer's *Letters and Papers from Prison!*

It was from those same letters, as it turned out, that I was given a perspective that informed me then—and now. His parents wrote to him, during the Christmas season, expressing their angst in celebrating the season knowing that he was living in such miserable conditions. He responded:

> We ought to find and love God in what He actually gives us; if it pleases Him to allow us to enjoy some overwhelming earthly happiness, we mustn't try to be more pious than God Himself and allow happiness to be corrupted by presumption and arrogance, and by unbridled religious fantasy which is never satisfied with what God gives. God will see to it that the man who finds Him in his earthly happiness and thanks Him for it does not lack reminder that earthly things are transient, that it is good for him to attune his heart to what is eternal, and that sooner or later there will be times when he can say in all sincerity, "I wish I were home." But everything has its time, and the main thing is that we keep in step with God.

I believe that this is what Lilias meant, in essence, when she wrote of being "*glad in His April days.*" She was speaking of the Christian life in its totality. She observes that it seems that, for some, the April days are seamless, "*where spring and summer weave the year between them, and the autumn processes are hardly noticed as they come and go.*" Her advice, echoed by Bonhoeffer's decades later, is that we should enjoy them "*while He gives them.*" After all, "*He is the God of the daisies and the lambs and the merry child hearts!*" (And, I might add, of birds and butterflies and bright blooming flowers!) April days, notwithstanding, "*The one thing is to keep obedient in spirit*" or, in Bonhoeffer's words, "the main thing is that we keep in step with God." Obedience. To "*be ready to let the flower-time pass if He bids.*"

In reality, most of us *do* experience winter, January days, figuratively speaking, sometimes for long stretches of time, with only a sprinkling of April days to brighten the spirit atmosphere. And it may be the memory of "flower times" past that sustains us, that gives us hope for better days to come.

Back to my rooms, my views . . . my April day in October. It is "*right to be glad in His April days while He gives them*"—be it a succession of days, a short April season, or an April moment. But I must hold lightly these very things that gladden my heart, today. I must embrace them as He intended: pointers to God, a glimpse of glory, a preview of heaven!

Lord, may I delight in all the blessings that gladden my heart today. May I hold lightly the same knowing that they are but a glimpse of glory that points to You.

Part 2

Images of God

The Dew of the Spirit

The grass has to stand very still as it holds its precious "weight of glory"—and so has the soul on whom the dew of the Spirit comes. Literally, as easily as this dew, His dew is brushed off—some of us know it to our cost. An impulse of impatience, a sense of hurry or worry allowed to touch us, a mere movement of the self-life against His checking and He is gone, and our soul stands stripped and bare. Noiseless must be His Holy Habitation within us.

—Diary June 30, 1885

Painting: from Travel Journal 1895

For our light affliction, which is but for a moment, worketh for us a far more exceeding and eternal weight of glory.   —2 Corinthians 4:17 KJV

FIVE WOMEN (one via conference phone!) meet for four days united in singleness of purpose. We have chosen a place, set apart, free from routine activity. The old-world charm and natural beauty of the historic inn promises the possibility of refreshment of body and of spirit.

We know what we hope to accomplish: to explore broader venues to

present and access the unique legacy of Lilias Trotter: art . . . writing . . . life . . .
We agree to the importance of her contribution—spiritual, artistic, ministry—
during her lifetime and recognize its significance in our own lives. We believe
her to be relevant today, to people aching for reasoned spiritual clarity, role
models, and meaning beyond themselves.

What we don't know is how and where God wants to use her—or us.
So we come humbly before God, seeking to ascertain and obey His bidding.
Toward that end, we dream and discuss and deliberate, then stand back, so to
speak, and release our thoughts to God's purposes. We search our hearts for
our motives and for indication of anything that could possibly impede the
work of God's Spirit in us and through us. Repeatedly. Throughout the week.

Home again, my new vision (beyond the task at hand) is a renewed desire
to be sensitive to "the dew of the Spirit." In a context solely devoted to a single
purpose, we were focused and intentional. Continually (and in community) we
returned to the stance of supplicant, conscious of anything that could brush
off the dew of the Spirit. But back, now, to the fragmented reality of my daily
life, it is so easy to forget. To become careless or indifferent or, dare I confess,
disobedient.

Lilias looked to the dew-bearing blades of grass. Absolute stillness was
requisite to hold its precious "weight of glory." The soul, on which the dew
of the Spirit comes, likewise, must remain still and quiet. She observes how
easily this "dew" can be brushed off: "*An impulse of impatience, a sense of hurry or
worry allowed to touch us, a mere movement of the self-life against His checking.*"

"*Noiseless must be His Holy Habitation within us.*" Challenged by Lilias's life
and words, I pray for stillness of heart—not only during those unique times
when consciousness is heightened by commitment and community, but daily
through personal desire and intention.

Spirit of the living God, fall afresh on me.

—Daniel Iverson

Our God Sees

Today's story is a very pretty one. The little pickle Melha went right up to her nearly blind father and pointed to one of the pictures on the wall—one of the Lord calling a little child to Him—and said, "Look at Jesus."

"I have no eyes O my daughter—I cannot see," was the answer.

The baby thing lifted head and eyes to the picture and said, "O Jesus, look at father!" Was that not a bit of heavenly wisdom? —July 28, 1909

Painting: Color plate from *Between the Desert & the Sea*

Are not two sparrows sold for a penny? Yet not one of them will fall to the ground outside your Father's care . . . So don't be afraid; you are worth more than many sparrows.   —Matthew 10:29, 31

THE BEST-SELLING book *Letters to God* was published in 1991, delighting a readership with children's directness, humor, and startling clarity of expression. For example, "Dear God, I do not think that anybody could be a better God. Well I just want you to know but I'm not just saying that because you are

God already. Charles." Perhaps more compelling, personally, are those candid conversations that arise spontaneously in the context of everyday living. Just as I treasured my own children's observations about God, now I relish accounts of *their* children's observations. ("Write them down," I warn my adult children. "You'll be surprised what you'll forget.")

An eight-year-old Kiersten, hiking a rocky hill, clasping her mother's hand as they climbed the steep terrain: "You are like Jesus to me—holding my hand and helping me. I feel safe with you."

A conversation overheard between six-year-old Davis and his four-year-old sister. "Audra, did you know that God can juggle houses?!" A nonchalant Audra, "Yeah, I know."

Children played an important role in Lilias's life. During her early years in Algeria, Lilias discovered that relationships with children gave her entrée to Arab families. Little gifts of bonbons for the children and pincushions for their mothers never failed to open their houses and their hearts. Later, through the decades, a parade of little girls came in and out of their home: some taking up permanent residency, others finding a bed off the street for the night. The pages of her diaries, illuminated with sketches and paintings, provide whimsical and tender vignettes of these irrepressible scamps, bringing joy (and challenges!) with their merry presence and disarming insight.

Little Melha was one such child. A wild bit of a girl, with dark eyes and long black lashes, she continually beguiled Lilias and her colleagues with her quaint ways and wise observations. With her simple request, "*O Jesus, look at father!*" she articulated a profound truth to her sightless father: the presence of an all-seeing God. So often a child receives in trust what we adults labor to believe. How can God possibly see us all at once? How can He keep everything within His sight or care? We attempt to reason out a mystery that confounds and transcends our human understanding. Yet throughout Scripture, this is affirmed: "The eyes of the LORD are everywhere" (Proverbs 15:3). "Nothing in all creation is hidden from his sight" (Hebrews 4:13). And "My eyes will watch over them for their good" (Jeremiah 24:6).

Perhaps that is why Jesus gathered children to Himself and upheld them as an example: "Let the little children come to me, and do not hinder them for the kingdom of God belongs to such as these. I tell you the truth, anyone who will not receive the kingdom God like a little child will never enter it." Certainly a logical God did not intend to frustrate our minds with inconsistency and illogic. At the same time, the created can never presume to fully comprehend the mind of the Creator. C. S. Lewis observed in *Mere Christianity*, "That is one of the reasons I believe in Christianity. It is a religion you could not have guessed. If it offered us just the kind of universe we had always expected, I should feel we were making it up. But, in fact, it is not the sort of thing anyone would have made up. It has just that queer twist about it that real things have."

An older couple, much afflicted by ill-health and immobility, was asked the secret of their bright hopefulness. Without hesitation the wife answered, "His eye is on the sparrow, and I know He watches me." Civilla Martin went home that evening and penned the verses of a simple gospel song, concluding with this joyful refrain: "I sing because I'm happy, I sing because I'm free, / For His eye is on the sparrow, and I know He watches me."

Lord, You love children and uphold them as an example.
Help me to accept the mysteries of faith with childlike trust in You.

Safe Am I

Can you not remember, my sister, as if it were yesterday, the hour your first born child lay in your arms and how your heart glowed with such love and joy that all you suffered in bearing it to life was forgotten. And as it lay there, weak and helpless, its very need called to you all the time, so that you could not forget it for a moment because of the great fountain of loving care that had sprung up in your heart. Even in the night you would wake at its faintest cry,

Painting: from Diary 1899

and put your arms round and care for its needs.

God created in you, my sister, that wonderful Mother heart, and He loves you with the same tender love that He has given you for your little ones, only far more tender and deep . . . you have a place of refuge in God as safe and warm and beautiful as you have ready for your child. Come and hide your head there when you are afraid of what may happen and if you are troubled bring your troubles there as your children come to you.

—Heavenly Light on the Daily Path
(privately published devotional for Arab women)

Can a mother forget the baby at her breast
    and have no compassion on the child she has borne?
Though she may forget, I will not forget you!   —Isaiah 49:15

As a mother comforts her child, so will I comfort you.—Isaiah 66:13

Once again, we experience the high point in the year family-wise, as we gather with our children and grandchildren, twenty-one strong, for seven wonderful days at the beach. It doesn't take long for the cousins to reconnect after a year's absence and reestablish relationships in various configurations. Soon relaxed vacation routines emerge: long hours at the beach ... late meals (lunches on the wrap-around porch, family dinners cooked, in turn, by each family unit) ... evening family time ... adult time (children bedded) when we talk late in the night (morning!) and share our stories of the year past.

It never ceases to amaze me how the children fill the sunny hours of the day, fueled by boundless energy and limitless imagination, beach and ocean providing the stage for play. I'm fascinated by shifting alliances—older children organizing activities ... younger children wandering off to build a sand castle or chase a crab ... the boys spending endless hours riding the surf ... Adults offer structure and the occasional verbal directive ("you're out too deep"; "let's put on more lotion"; "it's time to eat"; "be gentle with little Addie") as a background to the child-generated activity.

Until—there is a crisis! Stings from a jellyfish ... legs and arms attacked by sand fleas ... hurt feelings ... an unresolved argument ... possession rights challenged. Then cousins are instantly abandoned. The wounded child rushes to its parent, usually to a mother's lap. Often the comfort of a listening ear or a hug and kiss or a Band-Aid is sufficient, and a child is off and running again.

Lilias, ever seeking to find means to convey spiritual verities to the Arab women, seized on the maternal relationship to illustrate the heavenly Father's love in her self-published booklet *Heavenly Light on the Daily Path*. Illustrated with simple line drawings, she borrowed from the common, homely activities to illuminate heavenly truths: Writing in "The Lesson of the Mother's Lap": *"God created in you, my sister, that wonderful Mother heart, and He loves you with the same tender love that He has given you for your little ones, only far more tender and deep."* She underscored that truth with the Scripture passage of Isaiah 49:15 and Isaiah 66:13.

No less do we, as adults, need the comfort and reassurance of a heavenly Father. Nor are we, like our children, beyond the reach of our heavenly Father. We may be more sophisticated than our children in how we view our world, our expectations about God having been shaped by life experience and observation. We may not believe that all will turn out as we want, but rather understand that no matter what happens God will be there with us.

The challenge to convey, and accept, a personal and loving God was not unique to Lilias and her beloved Arab friends. Julian of Norwich (1342–1416) wrote *Revelations of Divine Love*, tender meditations on God's eternal and all-embracing love: "God is our clothing, who wraps and enfolds us for love, embraces us and shelters us, surrounds us with his love, which is so tender that he will never abandon us." She concludes her meditation with the reassurance that despite all the trials and sorrows faced by God's creation, in the end "all shall be well." All shall be well, because God constantly enfolds His creatures in His constant upholding love.

I look at our grandchildren, even our adult children, for that matter. How I long to embrace them, figuratively speaking, in my "mother lap"—to shield and shelter them from the inevitable sorrows of life. Yet I know that they will experience setbacks and suffering that no Band-Aid or hug or listening ear can assuage. Better by far to point them to their heavenly Father who is present for them in this world and will usher them safely into eternity.

A song they learned in Bible school—by Mildred Leightner Dillon— comes to my mind, replete with motions—hand covering a cupped palm: "Safe am I (safe am I) in the hollow of His hand."

Adult. Child.

You have a place of refuge in God—safe and warm and beautiful . . . Come and hide your head there when you are afraid of what may happen and if you are troubled bring the trouble there . . . when Satan tempts you or the world draws you run to your refuge . . . if the night of death comes before Jesus returns He will take you in His arms and hush your soul to sleep and you will know nothing more till you wake in the new day of heaven.

Thank You, Lord, for Your tender care.
Enfold me, and mine, in Your loving embrace.

Seeking Shepherd

I must put down a dear little story told me by a friend this morning. Her small niece, aged somewhere between three and four, was heard telling the parable of the lost sheep to a cousin a year or two older. The finale was, "So the Shepherd put back the lamb into the fold, and then He mended up the hole where it had got out." All of sanctification as well as salvation lay in the wisdom of those child-lips! —Diary May 28, 1926

Painting: a print on card stock

I myself will tend my sheep and have them lie down, declares the Sovereign LORD. I will search for the lost and bring back the strays. I will bind up the injured and strengthen the weak . . . I will shepherd the flock with justice. —Ezekiel 34:15–16

THE TRIPTYCH OF THE LOST SHEEP (Luke 15:1–7) was drawn by Lilias during her early years in North Africa. It wordlessly conveys a threefold message: lost, sought, found. But to fully appreciate the story, one must understand the context. Two groups of people had gathered around Jesus: the "good guys" (Pharisees and synagogue teachers); the "bad guys" (tax collectors and sinners). The religious group is offended by the fact that Jesus is eating with the "sinners," table fellowship being a sign of acceptance and friendship. Jesus's answer to their complaint is oblique. He tells three stories about three lost things: a lamb, a coin, a son.

The parable of the lost lamb aptly describes the character of sheep and of the shepherd. Sheep, by nature, are dumb, directionless, and defenseless. "By their very nature they need a shepherd," writes Charles Spurgeon, "and I suppose this is another reason why the figure of sheep is used to describe the relationship between the Lord and His people." In contrast to the religious leaders who shunned the "sinner," the Good Shepherd set off to find him. Jesus's heart ached for sinners, knowing they were, in truth, lost. The response to the lamb being found was to throw a party, one that reverberated in heaven! Jesus, the great Shepherd, makes the parallel: "There will be more rejoicing in heaven over one sinner who repents" (Luke 15:7).

The image of her heavenly Father as the loving shepherd was Lilias's favorite, the one to whom all her endeavors pointed. She was unceasingly drawn to the "lost lambs," whether the prostitutes of London's Victoria Station, the street urchins of Algiers, the cloistered woman of the Casbah, or the mystic brotherhoods of the Southlands. Often she shared this picture with individuals to reassure them that whatever their situation, however grave their sin, they had a shepherd whose heart would seek after them and would rejoice when they were safely back in the fold.

Lilias used this simple picture to illustrate a life-proven truth. I have reproduced multiple copies of it, one framed and placed on a shelf along with other images of the Good Shepherd; the rest at the ready to assure a hurting heart of the love of the endlessly seeking Shepherd. For who of us has not ached for a "lost" child or family member or friend or neighbor? Who of us has not, at one time or another, been that lost lamb? We can take comfort in the heart of a seeking—and caring—Savior.

O God, whose Son Jesus is the good shepherd of your people: Grant that when we hear his voice we may know him who calls us each by name.

—Book of Common Prayer

Spring of Life

How does a branch that is not a branch become one? By grafting. It must be severed from the plant on which it grew, and the severed surface is brought to a wounded place in the vine's stem, and bound there, heart to heart, and from the wounded place in the stem the sap flows out and seals the branch into union, and then it finds its way into the channels of the graft, and soon it needs no outward bonds to bind it there: it has become one with the vine.

—*The Sevenfold Secret*

Painting: Color plate from *Between the Desert & the Sea*

I am the vine; you are the branches. If you remain in me and I in you, you will bear much fruit.   —John 15:5

It was Jesus, really, who put this idea into personal terms the night before His crucifixion. John 15 relates an address to His disciples, in the upper room in which He draws them a beautiful word-picture of that relationship. But how, one might ask, can one that is a "branch" become one with the "Vine"?

This is a graphic picture for those of us who live in Central Florida, home of the citrus industry. Not long after we moved to Lake Wales, citrus growers informed me that Florida's orange crop is created from orange limbs grafted into native lemon root stock.

And so it is with the new life in Christ. We must be grafted into the vine that is Jesus. There is both a negative and positive aspect to such a union. Just as the old branch must be severed completely from its original source of life, we too must experience the "severance" from our "old life" through confession and repentance. However sharp and abrupt it may seem, we are ready for the grafting into the new life. We are bound to the vine, heart to heart, at the place where Jesus was wounded for us.

And this is just the beginning! As the sap flows freely from the vine to the branch, the Spirit of God flows freely into our hearts, through no effort of our own. Unless, of course, we clog or impede the flow by sin or indifference. *"It is utterly, unbelievably simple. Receive Jesus with a heart-grasp and you will find, like the flower, a spring of eternal life, entirely distinct from your own, set working deep down in your inmost being,"* Lilias wrote in *Parables of the Christ-life.*

What could be more desirable to a thirsty heart than an endless spring of life in one's inmost being, regardless of the parched or tired circumstances of one's outward existence?

The union is established, yes, but it is the beginning of new relationship, and like any relationship it requires nurture. Jesus concluded His teaching with a comforting implication of this new union: "I no longer call you servants . . . Instead I have called you friends" (John 15:15). Yes, we are joined in Christ, but now we have the unique privilege of abiding with Him, an ongoing process of knowing Him, of becoming more completely what He intended us to be: full persons. Whole.

I conclude where I began, with citrus, and a cautionary tale. For many years, after moving to Florida, I expressed my longing for a tangerine tree. It seemed to me the perfect fruit: sweet and accessible, the soft skin easily removed for instant enjoyment. One day, to my great joy, I discovered in a corner of our front lawn, yes, a tiny tangerine tree rich with the promise of future delights planted secretly (in the night?) by a good friend (and listener!) who was also in the citrus business. I watched it grow into a large symmetrical tree with glossy green leaves. It looked beautiful.

One day, several years later, said grower queried about my tree. "No fruit yet? Something's wrong with this tree." Then he threatened, "I'm going to smother the ground with fertilizer. If this doesn't work, I'm cutting it down."

I pled with him. I love this tree. It is beautiful. It provides shade and climbing for the children. He looked at me as if I were out of my mind: "That's all right for you to say. But I'm a citrus farmer. As far as I'm concerned, if it doesn't bear fruit, it's not doing its job. I'm cutting it down."

A happy ending to this story. It did bear fruit—for years and years. And it taught me a lesson. Citrus tree or branch, it exists to bear fruit: "*the power and sweetness of the vine flow into the branch that has lost its own life to find it in the new life which flows on till leaves and flowers and fruit appear.*"

Our true shelter and dwelling place is in Jesus, the eternal spring of life, who works within our inmost being. As we abide in that shelter, it becomes our true home, all the fibers of our heart locked in together with it, as the grafted branches abide in the vine, drawing from it the spring of life.

God, flow freely into my heart with Your life-giving Spirit.
May I, unimpeded by sin and self, bear fruit to glorify You.

Lesson of the Crab

I had a beautiful day alone at Pescade, in a fresh little cave that we had never found before. My sermon was from a little crab perched on a rock below, which matched his light-brown shell exactly. He was just as alive and just as happy whether basking the air and sunlight—or buried (as took place about every other minute) under a foot or two of water as a wave swept over him. I could see him though the clear green-ness, quietly holding on below. There is no place where it is difficult for Jesus to live. His life in us can be just as adaptable as the life He has given to this tiny creature. —Journal 1893

Painting: from Journal 1893

The Sovereign Lord is my strength,
>   he makes my feet like the feet of a deer,
>   he enables me to tread on the heights. —Habakkuk 3:19

It's Thursday already, and I have barely touched the projects intended for this week! Coming off the high of travel and family vacation and the elastic hours of summer, I was ready to press forward, this week, with a new and disciplined schedule.

The Plan: Address several back-burner writing assignments . . . tackle major household projects . . . catch up with my soul . . .

The Reality: Attend backed-up correspondence ... sift and sort piles of accumulated papers ... pick up doll boots and bonnets, and the remnants of grandchildren's creative play ... clear a refrigerator cluttered with three weeks' of unfinished food and drink ... and more.

Now the day is half spent, and productive working time has been swallowed by activities that can't be tallied. I tighten with inward pressure as I recalibrate the schedule to salvage the remaining hours. I worry: Will I meet my long-range deadlines if I can't even keep up with the simple tasks of today?

Once again, I remind myself, it is not what I'm doing, or *not* doing, that defines the value of my work or worth. It is who I am—*whose* I am—amidst all the clutter and seeming unproductivity of a given day. Furthermore, it is less what I am doing and more *how* I'm doing the inevitable "next thing" on my limitless list of "to do's."

I almost skipped my time alone, today, with God. Surely He understands. I can still talk to Him (pray on the run, so to speak), I reasoned. Moreover, my Scripture reading for today is in Habakkuk! What does the gloomy prophet (a minor one at that!) have to say to me?! But pause, I did, and he spoke directly to my heart:

"*There is no place where it is difficult for Jesus to live.*" He is present whether I'm "*basking the air and sunlight,*" ticking off one important thing after another in a superproductive life, or "*buried under a foot or two of water,*" washed by waves of unfinished tasks outwardly or discouragement inwardly.

The key is to be attentive to God. Attentive to His leading ... to His voice. He is present. Am I? He speaks. Am I listening? Or has all the din and clatter of my cluttered world muted His word and blocked His presence in my life? Wisdom of François Fenelon, from the seventeenth century, rings true today: "Be silent, and listen to God. Let your heart be in such a state of preparation that His Spirit may impress upon you such virtues as will please Him. Let all within you listen to Him."

There is no place where it is difficult for Jesus to live. His life in us can be just as adaptable as the life He has given the little crab—basking in air and sunlight or buried under a foot or two of water—*if we attend.* If we give Him room to live in us.

Just this week an event took place that commanded the attention of the most experienced or hardened journalists. Little did Antoinette Tuff know what another ordinary day as a bookkeeper at a Georgia elementary school would hold. But her heroic, clear-headed, compassionate dealing, single-handedly, with a deranged young man armed with five hundred rounds of ammunition calmed him into peaceful surrender, saving God knows how many lives of students, faculty, and police. Within twenty-four hours she was a proclaimed heroine in a personal telephone conversation with the president of the United States.

Admitting her inner terror—"I was actually praying in the inside. I was terrified but I was praying"—she walked through this event, a prime-time featured guest with CNN's Anderson Cooper, whose questions drew her to her pastor's Sunday sermon about being anchored in the Lord and His Word.

Would her story have had a different outcome had she not been "anchored"—rooted and grounded—in the Lord? Her life, by her own public admission, was not without challenges "devastating" in nature. But she was a vessel God could use for purposes she could not divine.

What about me? What am I missing when I keep plunging ahead with my frenetic activities—too busy, too distracted to attend? What might God be able to do with my life—with any life—if only we listened to and attended His voice, anchored in Him?

In his book of the same name, Richard Foster describes the place where Jesus lives as a "sanctuary of the soul." He says, "Throughout all life's motions—balancing the checkbook, vacuuming the floor, visiting with neighbors or business associates—there can be an inward attentiveness to the divine Whisper. The great masters of the interior life are overwhelmingly uniform in their witness to this reality . . . We bring the portable sanctuary into daily life."

There have been many reminders this week, amidst the clamor and clutter of living, to cultivate that place *"for Jesus to live,"* through times set aside, when possible and when not, to allow Him room to adapt within me, in the "portable sanctuary" of my heart.

Ever-present God, may I be attentive to Your presence. Come into the sanctuary of my heart and guide me in the acts and interactions of this day.

The Price of Power

Two glad Services are ours,
Both the Master loves to bless:
First we serve with all our powers
Then with all our helplessness.

Those lines of Charles Fox have rung in my head this last fortnight—and they link on with the wonderful words "weak with Him." For the world's salvation was not wrought out by the three years in which He went about doing good,

but in the three hours of darkness in which He hung, stripped and nailed, in uttermost exhaustion of spirit, soul and body—till His heart broke. So little wonder for us if the price of power is weakness.
　　　　　—Diary October 27, 1924

For to be sure, he was crucified in weakness, yet he lives by God's power. Likewise, we are weak in him, yet by God's power we will live with him in our dealings with you.　—2 Corinthians 13:4

Painting: from Diary 1904

AN ARMFUL OF FRESH FLOWERS—*"the wonderful deep crimson vetch that the French say first grew on Calvary"*—inspired Lilias to capture the beauty of a single sprig in watercolor. Her exquisite painting prompts my reflection on the account of Christ's impending death: what if He had lived a longer life on earth? Think of all the good that He accomplished in three years of ministry. Healing the sick . . . feeding the hungry . . . restoring dignity to the outcast . . . raising the dead . . . meeting the human heart at its point of need . . . Think about the host of people who could have been touched by His hands and His heart. Imagine the sheer number of people who would have rallied to His kingdom purposes.

Fact is, during His years of ministry, Jesus continually played down His power, discouraging people from broadcasting His works or acclaiming His name. He even silenced the three disciples who witnessed His celestial glory in the Transfiguration. It was not until the glory seemingly had passed and He appeared most vulnerable that Christ spoke, acknowledging explicitly His kingship and implicitly His divinity. Walter Wangerin in his Lenten reflections, *Reliving the Passion*, challenges: "Christian, come and look closely: it is when Jesus is humiliated, most seeming weak, bound and despised and alone and defeated that he finally answers the question, 'Are you the Christ?' Now, for the record, yes: I *am*. It is only in incontrovertible powerlessness that he finally links himself with power: 'And you will see the Son of man seated at the right hand of Power.'"

Yes, He could have lived longer. Despite the furor created by His very presence, God could have stayed the onslaught of His enemies. After all, God is all-powerful. Omnipotent.

The overruling reality remains: The central purpose of Christ's mission on earth was to die. Without His death there could be no resurrection life, for Him, for us. Without Good Friday there would be no Easter. "*The price of power is weakness.*"

All the good He did on earth, even at the height of His greatness (as we assess greatness) didn't compare with what He accomplished at the apparent point of defeat. It can be said without the slightest trace of exaggeration: "*The price of power is weakness.*"

What does this say to the so-called sanctified view of power often held by the church signified by size, structure, and program? More to the point, what does it say to *me*? Surely God asks—and blesses—service given from our strength: the fruit of all our powers. Stewardship. But perhaps an even greater service, one He especially blesses with His love and His power, is born out of our helplessness. Weakness.

Paul's challenge to the early church, beginning with Christ's incarnation and culminating at the cross, holds to this very day:

> Have the same mindset as Christ Jesus:
> Who, being in very nature God,
> > did not consider equality with God
> > something to be used to his own advantage;
> rather, he made himself nothing,
> > by taking the very nature of a servant,
> > being made in human likeness.
> And being found in appearance as a man,
> > he humbled himself
> > by becoming obedient to death—
> > even death on a cross!
>
> —Philippians 2:5–8

"So little wonder for us if the price of power is weakness."

God, You know my inadequacy in the face of formidable challenges. Please give me the courage to serve from my weakness, trusting that You will meet my weakness with Your strength.

Part 3

Images of Redemption

Harbinger of Spring

*The long hard winter has broken at last—not as yet in much sign on the
earthward side but in the late afternoon yesterday the great cumulus clouds sank
away, and in their place lay long horizontal bars, one above the other, dove-grey
touched with pale apricot, upon the tender eggshell blue of the eastern sky. They
are a harbinger of spring out here, that I have never known to fail.*

—Diary January 24, 1927

Painting: from Travel Journal 1894

See, I am doing a new thing!
Now it springs up; do you not perceive it? —Isaiah 43:19

SPRING RETURNS TO CENTRAL FLORIDA. Or at least first signs of the
same. While one could hardly call it a "hard long winter," compared to much
of our country, there definitely has been a period of dormancy punctuated with
stretches of chill even in our subtropical clime. So it is with a lift of joy that we
welcome signs of new life—"harbingers of spring"—that signal new beginnings:
tight new buds on our rose bushes, trees leafing out forcing off last season's
remnants of withered leaves, grass filling in bare patches with green, a tiny
yellow-bellied goldfinch flitting from branch to branch, trilling its song of praise.

And with spring comes a sense of renewal. The return of green and budding flowers brings a freshness of spirit and renewed energy. Some, like my mother, welcome spring with a brisk full-blown housecleaning, attic to basement, emptying bookcases and dusting each book, scrubbing walls and woodwork, washing windows and putting up screens, even switching out heavy drapery for gauzy organdy curtains to billow in the sweet spring breeze. Then the big finish: placing rich soil in old window boxes and filling them with young plants and fresh greenery.

I wonder if God intended the cycle of seasons to trigger within our spirits a like renewal. George Herbert in his beloved poem "The Flower" wrote: "How fresh, O Lord, how sweet and clean / Are thy returns! ev'n as the flowers in spring," suggesting that the same "returns" of His creation—"flowers in spring"—are possible in the souls of His creatures.

Surely God purposed us to see Him through His design—much as we see the artist through his or her consummate work, be it a building, a painting, a quilt.

One of the perks of researching the life of Lilias has been "conversations"— phone, e-mail, letter—with the few remaining people who knew her or knew people who did. Today I had yet another conversation with a woman in London who, with her husband, are the only living members of the original Algiers Mission Band. While they came to Algeria several decades after the death of Lilias, they lived in her home, Dar Naama, in the suburbs of Algiers. They worked with people who knew Lilias intimately, having served alongside her for many years.

At the end of our conversation, I put down my list of questions, and asked: "What would you like to tell me about Lilias? What would you want people to know?" She quickly said, "Love. Lilias was loved by the Arab people, and they knew that their 'La La Lily' loved them. But you can't talk about Lilias without noting her love of beauty, of nature. She rejoiced that God called her to a land of such beauty. And she believed that God's created order pointed back to the Creator—that we could learn about God through the beauty and design of His natural world."

"The world is charged with the grandeur of God," exulted Gerard Manley

Hopkins. He notes humanity's ill-treatment of the earth but concludes:

> And for all of this, nature is never spent:
> There lives the dearest freshness deep down things,
> And through the last lights of the black West went
> Oh, morning, at the brown brink eastward springs—
> Because the Holy Ghost over the bent
> World broods with warm breast and with ah! bright wings.

The rhythms of nature—night followed by day, the predictable seasons of each year—provide renewal and fresh starts in the physical world. They also suggest the same in the world of the spirit. Even as we open the windows of our houses to receive a fresh spring breeze, we can open the doors of our hearts to the refreshment that comes from the sweet breath of the Holy Spirit: *His* "nature never spent."

We know the bit of housecleaning our souls require, the refurbishing of our minds, the planting of new life in the spirit. Let us turn off our smart phones, take off our headphones, and be attentive to the world around us. What does God want us to see? What "new thing" does He want to do in our lives?

> The day is yours, and yours also the night;
> you established the sun and moon.
> It was you who set all the boundaries of the earth;
> you made both summer and winter.
>
> —Psalm 74:16–17

God, Your world gives constant testimony to Your design: renewal and rebirth throughout the changing seasons of the year. Renew and refresh my soul with the sweet breath of Your Spirit.

Glimmer of Light

In the garden there is an African "soldanella"—not a real soldanella—only an African version of the same truth of the wonders that God can do in secret. A garden border of a kind of thick matted grass, a foot high—so matted that the leaves were bleached yellow-white for want of sun, for a full third of their length. But right down below that level—almost on the ground—with barely a ray of light, its berries had ripened to wonderful sapphire blue-like jewels when one parted the mass and came upon them. Oh our God can do the same miracles with this tiny glimmer of light that comes to these souls in their tangle of darkness. Glory be to His name! —March 17, 1904

Painting: from Diary 1904

Let your light shine before men, that they may see your good deeds and praise your Father in heaven. —Matthew 5:16

IT HAD BEEN A DIFFICULT two and one half years for Lilias. Many of the advances in ministry had been curtailed by the French government's official resistance to all things English. On top of this was a sustained period of *"failure in sleeping powers & a sudden sense of having come to the end of my strength."*

Images of Faith ☆

Her return from her summer retreat in England to her beloved Algeria had been repeatedly postponed, and, even now back in Algiers, she lamented her "idleness." (The definition of which could be contested, given the various projects with which she was engaged!)

Perhaps her deepest discouragement was the setback in hopes for a station in Tolga, a Southland village where in 1900 they had been received with warm hospitality and open hearts. They returned two years later, greeted with the same welcome, and purchased a house for a winter station. Their delight was boundless as they furnished their own native home—with earthen walls and floor, ceiling of palm trunk and thatch of palm leaves—and received a steady stream of visitors. Then, without advance notice, their work was shut down by the French military commandant: "... *our hopes for steady work down here wrecked at a stroke—we fairly ached, body and soul, with the blow.*"

The one bit of encouragement came, without any outward sign of confirmation, through the "post" (an Algerian rider on horseback)—a passage from Proverbs, with the marginal note, "Surely there will be a sequel," which became a promise Lilias claimed of God. "*A glimmer of light.*" And she praised God for what she could not yet see.

In the city of Algiers, Lilias carried on the ministry, limited in her estimation, but formidable by any other standard: writing story parables in native phraseology; translating portions of the New Testament in colloquial Arabic, recruiting new workers from the Training Center in nearby Olivage.

It was here, at Olivage, that she observed the African "soldanella" with its brilliant blue berries surviving, even thriving, under improbable circumstances: hidden from the sun under thick matted grass. And, once again, God spoke to her through His creation. It spoke of the wonders God can do in secret . . . of the miracles God can do with a tiny glimmer of light.

It would be another twenty-one years before Lilias would witness the "sequel" she believed God had promised. Her return to the Southlands, first through the desert gates of El Kantara and then to the mud-walled town of Tolga, touched her heart as it had so many years before: "*Everywhere in the streets there are hands stretched out in welcome—gaunt hands of old men who were in their prime then, strong brown hands of middle-aged men who were but lads when we saw them last."* The mission home was reestablished. Lilias's love and vision for Tolga never waned, and long after she was unable to make the journey to the Southlands, the ministry continued for generations.

Lilias's trust in God's working through the "glimmers of light" that penetrated the improbabilities of sight sustained her through countless ministry challenges. While few of us would compare our kingdom work with Lilias's radical ministry, the reality of God's working is the same. I believe and take heart from the spiritual insights she derived in the battle zones.

I wonder, from time to time, just what difference my small efforts have made in the bigger scheme of things. Particularly those that were limited by time or circumstances. The promising student I taught for a year, never to see again . . . individuals who peopled my life, for a moment, not to know what has gone on since . . . the self-contained mission trip or church program that consumed a week or so . . . the chance conversation concerning spiritual verities . . . even efforts extended to family members who might not have fathomed the cost.

You can add your stories, whether employed "full-time" in ministry or living out faith, full time. How much of your time and energy has been expended on people, projects, or simple acts of service without the slightest indication of completion or results? We touch a life, invest our souls only to move on or have them move away from us. How often are we frustrated by the magnitude of the task and the limits of our contributions?

Yet! It is not really about our shedding of light. It is what *God* is doing with that glimmer of light. Oh, the wonders God can do in secret!

This is confirmed in my own life when I consider the glimmers of light that illuminated my life, often for only a brief time, often unacknowledged by me: the woman who built a childhood library for me, book by book, until I was ten years of age, and we moved a thousand miles away; the Bible teacher who brightened my first year of college with hospitality (tea and cookies) and led us through the book of Ephesians; two third-grade public-school teachers who mentored me through my first year among them; the authors who shaped my faith; older moms who informed my view of parenting and homemaking;

the two women who introduced Lilias to me and never knew what would evolve from their parting with their treasured books.

But I'm going to end where I started: with Lilias and the amazing "sequel" that prompted this reflection. Fast forward more than a century from the moment of despair when she claimed as from God "Surely there will be a sequel." Just this week I received an e-mail from a friend who met with a couple who had lived in Tolga! When she asked, "Have you ever heard of Lilias Trotter?" they answered a resounding yes. They had visited an Arab family in Tolga that mentioned a "Madame Lily" who had been a friend of their grandmother. This grandmother took classes from Madame Lily—food preparation and sanitation as well as needlework. She related how Lilias taught the girls to read—unheard of then—and even recalled Scripture verses that were since passed down through the generations. They credited her for modeling a tradition of hospitality for their family present to this day.

Lilias had no idea what of her loving efforts would be remembered. Nor do we. But of this she was certain—and so can we—that God would work His wonders in secret . . . that He would do miracles with tiny glimmers of light.

Lord, so much of my life is tending to little things with few obvious results. Take those tiny glimmers of light and work Your hidden wonders in the lives of others.

God's Workmanship

God builds up a shrine within us of His workmanship, from the day in which Jesus was received. The seed-vessel is its picture. With the old nature He can have nothing to do except to deliver it to death: no improving can fit it for His purpose, any more than the leaf or tendril however beautiful, can be the receptacle of the seed. There must be "a new creation," "the new man," to be the temple of the Divine Life. —Parables of the Christ-life

Painting: from *Parables of the Christ-life*

For we are God's workmanship, created in Christ Jesus to do good works, which God prepared in advance for us to do.

—Ephesians 2:10

I<small>T</small> WAS THE SUMMER OF 1983. We were working our way up the eastern coast, stopping at B&Bs along the way, toward our destination: a family reunion on Cape Cod. As we were skirting Washington, D.C., Dave succumbed to my pleas to stop at the Washington National Cathedral. "Just one hour. Promise"—to fulfill my dream of seeing the then recently completed *Ex Nihilo* creation tympanum over the main doors of the west facade.

This sculpture had taken my heart from the first article I read about Frederick Hart's prize-winning design for the portrayal of the biblical creation. The eight "unfinished" figures emerging from stone, writhing with the agony of "being created," touched a deep place in my soul. It had been, for me, a challenging year on several fronts, and somehow this sculpture captured the very quiddity of the ongoing work of creation, making sense of what were, in reality, "trials" not "tribulations."

The children were only too glad to have an hour outside the confines of the car. Dave found a bench on which to read and nap. I was alone, on pilgrimage, and even if only for one hour, I was at liberty to study this masterpiece within a massive arch, towering above the great double doors of the cathedral.

It did not disappoint. Most compelling to me was the sculptor's vision of creation not as a finished work but as a process: a state of becoming. Evident in the figures and faces of force and beauty was struggle: bodies emerging out of the nothingness of chaos caught in a moment of transformation. Frederick Hart, in his own words, conceived his creation sculpture "as an eloquent metaphor for humankind always 'becoming,' ever in a state of rebirth and reaffirmation of all the possibilities in being human."

Time up. I purchased postcards of the creation tympanum, souvenir of these sacred moments and a reminder of the life-giving message inherent in those unfinished figures emerging from stone. Being created. *Becoming.* Years later I purchased a facsimile of the same, and mounted it over the lintel of our dining room doorway, under which I pass countless times a day.

Becoming. It might have taken the visual shock of seeing it demonstrated in stone to penetrate my dulled sensibilities, but it is a fundamental teaching of Scripture: "For we are God's workmanship, created in Christ Jesus to do good works, which God prepared in advance for us to do" (Ephesians 2:10). We are *being* created.

And in that recognition is both hope and caution. Hope: I am not a finished product. There's opportunity for improvement. Caution: It's not about *me.* It's not about me growing toward wholeness for random personal purposes or gain. We're *being* created "to do good works, which God has prepared in advance for us to do."

God, the master stonecutter, is continually at work, chipping and shaping His creatures into the beings He intended us to be. Some of the finished product is determined, at start, by the substance out of which we are being created. But the individuality, the specificity, is being determined by the skillful and purposeful hand of the Creator.

There is a limit, of course, as to how far one stretches the analogy. After all, unlike the soulless stone, we can resist the Sculptor's design. But there are many parallels to point out. The most obvious being, we did not make ourselves. We are the creation of something—Someone—regardless of the human processes that brought us into being. Second, while much of our growth occurs slowly, cell by cell, much shaping is requisite to make us fully formed human beings, reaching our full potential. Furthermore, much of the refinement of our souls has come as the result of the trials and testing that felt, at the time, like the sharp chisel of the stonecutter.

Speaking personally, I can look back over my life and acknowledge growth that came simply from the maturing process of age and experience. But, if I am completely honest with myself, my periods of greatest progress—growth—have come as a result of being tested and tried beyond my comfort zone: experiences that required more from me than I could personally resource; situations that ultimately (sometimes as a last resort) threw me into the arms of God. I would never choose the challenges or setbacks. Some hurt terribly, and I recoil from the blows. But I do have a choice to submit my life—with its inevitable challenges— into the hand of the Sculptor for His refining work.

In one of George MacDonald's books, a character named Dorothy proposes that a Mrs. Faber is "quarreling with the process" of God's craftsmanship. If only we would consent to the process, allowing the Creator to use daily joys and challenges for our formation, yes, but submitting to the chisel as well, knowing its sharp blows to be essential to the shaping of our souls—"*the temple of the Divine Life.*"

God's workmanship or ours? The choice is up to us!

God, I am Your workmanship, a work in process. Sculpt me into
the person You intend me to be, to fulfill Your purposes for my life.

The Myrrh of Heartbrokenness

The gathering of the bitter-sweet myrrh of heartbrokenness over failure and shortcomings—over all the "might-have-been's" of the past—can bring one nearer heaven than the gathering of frankincense of the hills, for present and future. Such is His abounding grace, even when sin has abounded. The place where we wash His Feet with our tears has a great nearness to His Holy place.

—Diary March 14, 1926

Painting: from Diary 1907

Now you must repent and turn to God so that your sins may be wiped out that time after time your soul may know the refreshment that comes from the presence of God. —Acts 3:19 PHILLIPS

I'M AN IDEALIST. I admit it. Some might say a romanticist. I grew up with *Anne of Green Gables* and *Little Women* and built around myself an "idealized world" of beauty and goodness. And while I never was taught this bit of practical theology—much less worded it as such—it amounted to something like this: "If

I do my best to live a good Christian life, if I cover each problem with prayer, God will spare me life's tragedies. Sure, I will face trials and testings (necessary for growth), but in the final analysis God will deliver those who love and serve Him." In short, a fairy-tale ending: "they lived happily ever after." Although this idea had its obvious flaws, it carried me through the ups and downs of childhood and well into my youth.

Then three crises converged, the summer between my sophomore and junior years of college, for which my Christian worldview was inadequate; crises involving death, financial reverses, and a life-changing family situation for a beloved cousin. Each situation touched my life deeply and had tremendous implications for all involved. And they all shared common ground: the fervent but seemingly unanswered prayers of godly people.

For the first time I was witnessing Christians with faith and experience far greater than mine go through situations that had no perceived happy ending. My first response was grief. For those I loved. For me—innocence lost. And then in time, grief was replaced with a kind of shadowy anxiety. How could I— how could anyone—be safe in a world that was not a respecter of persons?

Rare is the person who will sail through life without challenge. (Of course I was fortunate to have reached my late teens without having experienced significant trauma.) Sooner or later, there comes a time when the props that hold up our small crafts are insufficient. The death of a loved one. A betrayal. A physical disability. A personal failing.

The Bible is a story of broken dreams, dashed hopes, failures, and disappointments. Human failing is a thread running through the Old and New Testaments. But it is, above all, a book about redemption. God redeeming human failure, pain, and loss. It is the story of hope and fresh starts.

One of my favorite stories is about Joseph, who had more than his fair share of disappointments, betrayal, and setbacks. From Joseph, facing head-on the brothers who betrayed him, thus setting off the series of events that would lead him to being Pharaoh's second in command, we first hear these now-famous words: "You intended to harm me, but God intended it for good" (Genesis 50:20).

Isn't that the story of redemption? Taking something bad and turning it for good? Slavery for freedom: physical and spiritual. *Redemption* is a multifaceted word with many implications, but for much of my life I understood "redemption" as exclusive to salvation: once and for all, my sins were redeemed on the cross, Christ paying the cost, His life for mine.

And that, indeed, is a rich and fundamental doctrine of Christianity. But I've come to see that it is that—and more. God is continually involved in our redemption. He is in the business of an ongoing redemption in the life of each Christian, continually taking the bad and using it for good—if released to Him for that purpose.

What about those things that I have done wrong—from weakness or lack of intention or, worse, deliberation? What about actions or failings that may have long-term effects on others: my children, my friends? Looking back, I can see my mistakes, my failings, but what does one do when it is too late, when the damage—to myself or others—is beyond repair?

This story speaks, at slant, to questions in my heart: In the workshop of a great Italian artist, a young servant cleaned the studio every evening. One day he timidly asked, "Please, sir, would it be all right if I saved for myself the bits of broken glass you throw on the floor?"

"Do as you please; they are of no use to me."

For years the young man faithfully carried out his task. Every day he sifted through the discarded bits of glass, setting some aside.

One day the craftsman entered a back storeroom and came across a carefully hidden piece of art. Bringing it to the light and dazzled by its brilliance, he asked the servant, "What is the meaning of this? What great artist has hidden his masterpiece here?"

"Master," he replied, "don't you remember? You said I could have the glass you threw to the floor. These are the broken pieces" (adapted from *Mountain Trailways*, by Mrs. Charles Cowman).

God is the great redeemer of all circumstances. There is no situation resulting from either sin or ignorance that is beyond His reconstruction. While neither we, nor sometimes others, can escape the consequences of our actions, when we turn to Him with a humble heart, "*washing His Feet with our tears*," and release to Him the shattered segments of our lives, He will take those broken pieces and make from them something good.

We cannot deny the existence of brokenness or the corresponding pain and hurt, yet there is nothing to be gained in staring at the broken pieces. Once we have, in true repentance, turned from our error, making every possible reparation, we must gather the fractured fragments and give them once and for all to the One who has promised to work all things for the good of those who love Him. The final design may not be what it would have been; the individual parts may be imperfect, yet the great Redeemer can take all the pieces and make from them a work of art excelling our human imaginings. "Redemption, in its deepest sense," wrote Alister McGrath in *Redemption*, "is about being accepted as we are, while being transformed into what we are meant to be."

"And we know that in all things God works for the good of those who love him, who have been called according to his purpose" (Romans 8:28).

᠅ ᠅ ᠅

God, You alone know the frailty and failures of my faithless heart.
Please take the broken pieces, washed with tears of repentance,
and redeem them for Your purposes.

Beauty from Brokenness

Conscious weakness as a preparation for service is one thing; brokenness is another. We may know that we are but earthen pitchers, like Gideon's, with nothing of our own but the light within, and yet we may not have passed through the shattering that sets the light forth. It is an indefinable thing, this brokenness, and it is unmistakable when it has been wrought.

—Parables of the Christ-life

And we know that in all things God works for the good of those who love him, who have been called according to his purpose.   —Romans 8:28

Waiting her turn.

Painting: from Journal 1898

TWO PEOPLE E-MAILED ME an article, "Beauty Restored." Both for the same reason. It reminded them of Lilias.

It was inspired by the *New York Times* op-ed article in which Angelina Jolie went public with her announcement of her preventative double mastectomy. The writer, Brian Draper, noted her bravery in "not hiding the scars of her own recent breakage and reconstruction." He went on to describe an ancient Japanese craft, *kintsugi*. When a valuable piece of china was dropped and broken, instead of throwing it away or repairing it, the craftspeople pieced it together with a lacquer mixed with gold. "And the restored item was considered far more beautiful than the original—because of its brokenness."

Brokenness. We live in a throw-away culture that denies or rejects imperfection. In things. In persons. Something breaks, we throw it away and replace it with something new. Someone is broken or imperfect. That person is shunned or sidelined, aborted or euthanized.

Yet no one is protected from or impervious to brokenness. At start, no one is born perfect. It is only a matter of time before something will mar any illusion we might have of perfection. Brokenness is our reality, regardless of cause: our own faults or failings . . . the result of another's abuse or carelessness, intentional or otherwise . . . or simply the reality of our existence in a broken world.

Indeed, it was into just such a broken world that Perfection came, taking on human form: to identify with us, to walk alongside us, to bear and heal our wounds, to be broken Himself, ultimately, in order to redeem and restore us. *Kintsugi.* Love is the gold-infused lacquer transmuting brokenness to wholeness and beauty.

Redemption: grace extended. Proof perfect that even in our very brokenness we are worth something. Worth restoring. *Kintsugi.* Thank God, He is not a deity with a throw-away mentality!

Lilias, in *Parables of the Christ-life,* refers to the Old Testament story of Gideon sending his men to battle, in the dead of night, equipped only with a sword and an earthen pitcher. Not until the pitchers were shattered could the candles within shine forth and illuminate their steps. In *A Path through Suffering,* Elisabeth Elliot noted, "The light is shed abroad because the vessel is broken."

Shattered. Broken. From that very brokenness God can make something of true beauty. We can choose to finger the fractured fragments of our lives scrutinizing them with self-reproach or bitterness. Or we can release them to God and view the emerging masterpiece being recreated by the skillful hands of the master craftsman.

God, we are broken people in a broken world. Take the brokenness of my life and heal it with Your life-restoring love.

Stored Energy

There is something wonderful in the thought that all the world's commerce of late, and much of the political movements that stand co-related hang on the coal supply; in other words, on bringing to the surface the buried lives of the trees and plants of ages far away. May it not be that just as unlooked for results in ages to come may spring from souls that "lay in dust, life's glory dead," and have before them "a better resurrection" in power transmuted in undreamed of ways when God's purpose come to birth. The buried fronds and fibres seemed over and done with, but their stored-up sunrays were waiting undimmed through those centuries on centuries of burial, only waiting to be given out.

—I. Lilias Trotter, Pigott

Painting: from Pocket Sketchbook 1877

He who began a good work in you will carry it on
to completion until the day of Christ Jesus.   —Philippians 1:6

IT WOULD BE MORE RELEVANT, today, to use the analogy of *oil* to demonstrate the political and economic currency of buried energy, but the point is well taken even after one hundred years. Coal has been called "buried sunshine," because the plants that formed it captured energy from the sun to create the plant tissues and, in turn, carbon that gives most of its energy.

Lilias, as always, found lessons in nature that spoke to spiritual realities. Coal spoke to her of unlooked-for results from the efforts of people from time past: " *'a better resurrection' in power transmuted in undreamed of ways when God's purpose come to birth.*"

I'll never forget the impact on those words when I first read them in Blanche Pigott's compilation of Lilias's letters and journals, *I. Lilias Trotter.* I was slowly—to make it last longer—working my way through the big brown book, savoring every bit of Lilias's wisdom and perspective. It came at a time when I was longing for encouragement that transcended the passing trends of conflicting methods and approaches to ministry. For that matter, approaches to *life.* As I read these life-giving trend-silencing words from a writer virtually unknown to me, I knew that God had gifted me this person from another time and place to speak eternal verities into my parched soul.

"*The buried fronds and fibres seemed over and done with, but their stored-up sunrays were waiting undimmed through those centuries on centuries of burial, only waiting to be given out.*" Her "sunrays" were buried only a century, in contrast to the possible millions of years needed to produce the "*buried sunshine*" of coal, but I felt at that moment that her words were "*waiting undimmed*" for this one needy person! Little could I then have imagined what "God's purposes" were for me concerning the "giving out" of that energy to others!

Since then, I've thought often of this principle of stored energy from things (and people) past and present—for God's purposes in God's time. And it begs the question: what am I doing now that might have consequences for the future? We see this a bit with our progeny: in the normal course of events, our children will outlive us. We will never know fully the effects of our training and example on their lives or even their impact on others'. Perhaps we've consciously invested in something much bigger than ourselves: a church, a company, a building, a project, a work of art ... We don't know the results of those efforts in a future with, or without, ourselves. It's a bit like Nelson Henderson's adage: "The true meaning of life is to plant trees under whose shade you do not expect to sit."

Sometimes this is easier to perceive with hindsight. I think of Werner Burklin, son of missionaries to China, who saw his parents' ministry shut down; under house arrest for five years, they were eventually forced out of the country. They would never know that, decades later, their son and then their grandson would return to the very province where they first lived, to provide leadership training and materials for countless Chinese pastors ministering to millions of national Christians. "*Stored-up sunrays waiting undimmed*" through the years "*only waiting to be given out.*"

Less spectacular, but no less providential, my husband and I have been privileged, throughout four decades of parish ministry, to witness individuals who late in life have come into a personal relationship with Jesus. Often, part of their story is an account of a parent or grandparent who prayed for them yet never knew of their commitment. "*Stored-up sunrays waiting undimmed through the years, only waiting to be given out.*"

Tree or coal notwithstanding, we are by nature creatures of the here and now: what you see is what you get. We live in a culture that craves and promotes instant gratification: You don't witness results? Go on to something more productive. Now.

But what have we missed when driven by results, alone? Is it possible we have lost the bigger picture in which God wants us to play a significant, if unnoticed, part? Perhaps it comes, in part, from our limited understanding of time? In *Mere Christianity*, C. S. Lewis suggests that our concept of time is quite different from God's: "Almost certainly God is not in Time. His life does not consist of moments following one another . . . every other moment from the beginning of the world—is always the Present for Him . . . He has all of eternity in which to listen."

Lilias, as much a strategist as she was, acted fully in the present, listening and waiting on God to do His bidding. She left the "results" to Him. "His time, His way" was a constant thread throughout the pages of her journals and published writings.

The thrill that I experienced in the first reading of this Lilias quotation came back in stronger power as I was preparing to write her biography. Could it be that I was part of that bigger plan to introduce, a century later, her timeless perspective to a time-driven generation? "*Stored-up sunrays waiting undimmed . . . only waiting to be given out.*"

Time is nothing to God: nothing in its speeding; nothing in its halting. He is the God that "inhabiteth eternity."   —December 12, 1920

➙ ➙ ➙

Lord, I am so earthbound, so consumed in the here and now. Free me from the pursuit of results to the higher calling of faithfulness.

The Pain of Parting

There is a wonderful sense of expansion—endless expansion—about our love for those who are gone, as if it had escaped earthly fettering. The pain of the parting is just the rending of the sheath, as it were, to let the flower have its way. And their love for us will have grown in the same way, only in fuller measure, into something pure and fathomless and boundless and inexhaustible because it is "in God." —Diary May 26, 1918

Painting: from Algerian Pocket Sketchbook 1888

Great is thy faithfulness. The LORD is my portion, saith my soul; therefore will I hope in him. The LORD is good unto them that wait for him, to the soul that seeketh him. —Lamentations 3:23–25 KJV

ONE YEAR AGO THIS WEEK, my mother went to the "Home" for which she longed. This first anniversary of her death brings to the surface vivid memories of the last months of her ninety-eight years.

Telephone calls had become almost a daily ritual. Often my creativity was challenged by "topics to talk about" as her world became increasingly limited (along with her hearing). There was something that would inevitably resonate: a shared memory . . . a Scripture verse . . . favorite songs sung, in duet, over the miles . . . events in her life (a health flare-up, a visit or letter, flowers outside her window, sometimes a tidbit of breaking news) . . . events in the lives of her grandchildren and great-grands, as she loved to call them.

Often our conversation would end with a prayer. "What would you like me to pray for you?" I would ask this person who had faithfully prayed for me (and mine) through the decades of my life. I would brace myself for what was becoming her stock answer: "Pray that God would take me Home." Stab to heart. I'd try to affirm her value. Now. Her prayers, her listening heart, her simply "being there" for her family, for *me* in recent transitions, her continuing to pioneer each life stage, modeling now what it looks like to "grow old gracefully." When my attempts seemed less than convincing, I would tease, "Well, I guess God just isn't ready for you quite yet." Invariably that would bring a rueful chuckle, "I guess not."

And so it was, one evening, the same routine, but this time with a surprise twist. To my "what do you want me to pray for you?" she paused, drew a deep breath, and answered, "Pray for me to have courage." Was it a health crisis she feared? Death? "Courage for what?" I asked. "Courage for *living*."

Courage for living. Is that not really the challenge we all face to one degree or another and in various forms? Joan Chittister observed in *Illuminated Life*, "One of the most difficult, but most seasoning elements of life is simply the fine art of getting up every morning, of doing what must be done if for no other reason than that it is our responsibility to do it. To face the elements of the day and keep on going takes a peculiar kind of courage. It is in dailiness that we prove our mettle. And it is not easy."

There are so many escape routes from, well, life. As a culture we have become escape artists from reality, numbing our feelings in substances or activities or people or things. We look for ways to avoid the source of our fears by skirting around the issues at hand or denying their very existence. Often it is only when we have no other option that we are forced to look at our circumstances and ourselves confronting, at last, what it is that we fear.

My brother identifies "Life's Two Greatest Fears"—dying and living—in a sermon by the same name. I am grateful that we have had the privilege of having a mother who lived long enough to show her adult children both how to live and how to die. With *courage*. Whether it was in the big trials and tests of life or merely the tedium of seemingly endless days. Courage.

At the end of the day—literally our days on earth—comes "*a wonderful sense of expansion*"—the "*endless expansion*" of eternity with God. "He will wipe every tear from their eyes. There will be no more death or mourning or crying or pain" (Revelation 21:4). Yes, Mother has escaped earthly fettering, at last. And "*the pain of the parting is just the rending of the sheath, as it were, to let the flower have its way*"—to let her Savior have His sway.

Thank You, God, for providing for me a model of courage.
Strengthen me to face my fears of living and help me to view
the challenges of earth in the light of eternity.

Part 4

Images of
Spiritual Growth

August Oranges

All little miniature beginnings but all "beautiful in their time," like the dark green August oranges in the court below. The fact that they have got thus far into being is more than a promise. Like all the promises of God they are (given the conditions) an accomplishment begun. "His 'Yea' only waits our 'Amen.'"

—Diary August 11, 1906

FRIDAY, AUGUST 10.

August Oranges.

Painting: from Diary August 10, 1906

He has made everything beautiful in its time.   —Ecclesiastes 3:11

I GAZE AT THE PICTURE posted on our daughter's Facebook wall. Three tow-haired children, toasted brown by the summer sun, freshly scrubbed, hair brushed and clad in brand new clothes—ready for their first day of school. They are sitting at the kitchen table, name holders identifying their place by their new classes: 6th Grader; 4th Grader; 1st Grader. Such an attitude of expectancy. Fresh start. New beginning.

There is something about new beginnings! Evelyn Bence captures the spirit of expectancy in the prologue of her compilation *New Beginnings: Celebrate the Fresh Starts of Life*:

> A new beginning. A fresh start. A clean slate. There is something almost irresistible about a new beginning: Whether it's starting a new job, moving into a new home, enrolling in a new school, or beginning a new relationship, a new venture makes you feel like a child on the first day of school. Armed with a fistful of newly sharpened pencils and an unsoiled notebook tucked under your arm, you stand prepared for the new adventure. Your stomach flutters with anticipation as you face new challenges and new lessons. Lessons of courage and valor, perhaps. Certainly lessons of achievement and failure. But above all else, a new beginning represents hope.

Hope! There is something about new beginnings that appeals to a universal (if latent) sense of hope. It holds the promise of something more—or different. A new chance. Change. Look at newness in nature: a seed, a bud, a sapling. Consider the same in humankind: a dream, a project, a job, a location. Perhaps we see it most in a newborn baby, untouched by life yet brimming with possibilities.

I remember holding our third (and last) newborn in my arms, listening to the song "I Am a Promise" on a Gaither Trio record (yes, record!) given to me by my mother. Perhaps it was the season (Christmas) or maybe hormones, but I was overcome with emotion as I considered the unknown possibilities in this little bundle of humanity: "You are a promise to be anything God wants you to be."

New beginnings signal all the above: possibility . . . promise . . . potentiality. This was the sermon the *dark green August oranges* preached to

Lilias toward the end of what was arguably the three most difficult years in Algiers. The local government continually sabotaged their ministry through varied and creative forms of oppression, severely limiting their programs and reducing the involvement of the Arab people. Lilias's compromised health forced an extended period of rest away from the rigors of Algiers and, even upon return, months of continuing weakness limited her activities. There were disappointments with the closest of their Arab friends.

Yet even in the darkest months of unrelenting difficulty, inward and outward, there were rays of hope: *dark green August oranges* holding more than a promise in their new beginnings. First, there was an advance in literature: developing story parables firmly set in the context and customs of Algeria as well as a revision of parts of the New Testament into a truly colloquial Arabic.

Then, even more amazingly, came the opportunity to buy an old native house, in the nearby suburb of El Biar, at a sum only slightly greater than the less adequate cottage they sought for relief from the summer heat and humidity. Lilias viewed the rambling house crowning the hillside of vineyards and firwood and reveled in the possibilities for the future: a training center, a halfway house for fledgling believers, rallies for Christian workers, guest rooms for weary workers. "*It seemed like a fairy tale of dreams suddenly dropped down to earth—yet with a curious sense that it was no dream but a wonderful bit of God's unfoldings . . . Such visions come of what God might make of it—& the only answer I get when I ask Him what it means is 'He Himself knew what He would do.'*"

Dark green August oranges—time alone would fully reveal God's plan but "*the fact that they got thus far into being is more than a promise of what was to come.*" Each individual "orange" indicated the promise of work begun and, "*like all the promises of God they are (given the conditions) an accomplishment begun.*"

Life is growth and change. It is never static. God has purposes and promises for what He intends for our lives. If only we listen. And are patient. We must faithfully tend the "dark green oranges"—not disparaging their size and color—as they are more than a promise of an accomplishment begun.

The key, I believe, is in the rest of the simple song, which encourages us to "listen to God's voice" with the assurance that we will "hear God's voice" and that He will help us to "make the right choice." The underlying message: with God's help we "can be anything God wants us to be." And, I would add, do anything He wants us to do. When we are attuned to God's voice, present to His Spirit then, as Lilias writes, "*His 'Yea' only waits our 'Amen.'*"

What are the *dark green August oranges* in my life? In your life? The beginning of a relationship . . . a new job . . . a move to a new location . . . the start (or restart) of a project or ministry . . . perhaps it is a new approach to an old situation or relationship . . . the embrace of a dream deferred. "*All little miniature beginnings are 'beautiful in their time,' like the dark green August oranges . . ..Like all the promises of God they are (given the conditions) an accomplishment begun.*"

Lord, how I love fresh starts and new beginnings! May I tend faithfully the "small green oranges" in my life and trust You for the fulfillment of their inherent promise.

Growing Points

Growing points were the things that spoke to me on the journey through Italy. You can see them already on the bare boughs, waiting for the spring, and all the year through they are the most precious thing the plant has got, be it great or small, and the most shielded therefore from chance of harm. And the growing point of our soul is the thing with which the Spirit of God is specially dealing, and all depends on faithfulness there. —Diary August 11, 1906

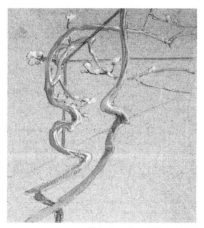

Painting: from Diary 1904

Forget the former things; do not dwell on the past.
See, I am doing a new thing! Now it springs up; do you not perceive it?
I am making a way in the wilderness and streams in the wasteland.

—Isaiah 43:18–19

ONE OF THE GREAT and unexpected joys of retirement has been gardening— Dave tending; I cutting!—spurred, no doubt, by having been gifted a rose garden. Eight rose plants bring delight whether viewed outside or framed by the dining room window. Foliage or bloom, each aspect provides recreation: tilling the soil, tending the plants, watching buds unfurl to flower, choosing the perfect moment to cut and capture the blossom for display in silver bud vase or flask of cranberry glass.

Perhaps one of the prime pleasures, for Gardener Dave, is the daily examination of each individual bush for signs of new life: flush of red foliage signaling the advent of new buds. Daily, in season (almost year-round in Florida) he proudly proclaims the promise encapsulated in sheaths of green: ten buds . . . twenty-two buds . . . sixty-three buds! Each bud signals new life. Growing points. Each new growing point, whether a rose or any other plant, signals the same: hope, potential, promise. *Life.*

And as it is with the plant, so it is with the soul. Each new growing point indicates life. Many years ago I read a book by Bruce Larson, *Living on the Growing Edge.* The title has challenged me to this day. Larson observed a remarkable teacher known not only for her effective teaching of young students, but for her ability to help them understand themselves and life. He asked her about her method. She explained that she tried to be aware of the "growing edge" of each student. The growing edge, it seems, is that area where the student is ready and able to learn. A good teacher must know what a student needs to learn and is ready to learn, and then present the student with that material.

Larson makes his point:

> Surely this is how the Holy Spirit wants to work in each of our lives. Every one of us has a spiritual growing edge. We all have mastered certain skills and subjects and disciplines and formed certain attitudes. Our tendency is to sit back and make this the sum and substance of the Christian experience. On the other hand God says, "Well done," and then moves us on to new areas that we can grasp and master.

It is, in reality, much easier to stay put, so to speak, to play to the middle ground of one's particular area of strength. Maybe, even a bit smugly, measure others by that strength and come out winning. But growth, real growth, is pushing out to the edge of our experience—to our personal growing edge—out of our safety zone into new life. In the realm of art, it has been said that an artist never stands still. One is either growing or dying. The same could be said in the life of the soul. Faith that huddles in the security of the known is a faith that repeats itself, without moving out to the edge, toward God's even greater intentions for us.

Countless examples in every disciple illustrate this concept. But here I think of my mother in the final decade of her life. Old-school, by generation and temperament, she gloried in her role as "support partner" to her husband. We as a family watched her redefine her role, to accommodate her husband's failing health, taking the lead for herself and her mate. Then as a widow she restructured her world, to better connect with her geographically scattered family. She remembered the names of her sixteen great-grandchildren by group photos from which she prayed for them. At age ninety-two she started writing her memoirs, to impart her legacy of faith to her family. While I knew that she kept up with world and national events, it wasn't until her memorial service that I learned the scope of her reading. She read the sports pages of the *Chicago Tribune*, just to keep informed and conversant with her grandson-in-law's interest in the Pittsburgh Steelers. She passed along her copy of *Psychology for Living* to another grandson-in-law who was a clinical psychologist.

"Living on the growing edge" will mean different things to different people. It will mean different things for the same person at various seasons of life. For my mother, an introvert by nature, it meant pushing herself in many directions to connect with her family and remain active in an increasingly foreign world. The growing point of a soul may be, like Mother's, determined by response to a radical life event . . . it might be opening oneself to a challenging experience or point of view; it could be developing a new skill to open new doors of opportunity, or swallowing one's pride by releasing one's "right to be right" for the restoration of a relationship. It might require embracing new ways of doing things in music or worship . . . taking a risk, even in the face of possible failure . . . being more active if we are reflective by bent or vice versa.

Living on the growing edge. Growing points. At the end of the day, it is not a senseless arbitrary action, jumping to the unknown or untried. Rather, it is being attentive to the working of God's Spirit in our souls. *"The growing edge of our soul is the thing with which the Spirit of God is specially dealing and all depends on faithfulness there."*

Lord, reveal to me the growing points of my soul. Help me not to be stuck in the security of the past but to be open to change and growth.

How Silently, So Silently

*All that outworking of His Grace has come so silently—"not with
observation"—like His work in all growth around—so that one can hardly
tell when or how the expansion has come.* —Diary March 9, 1923

Painting: from Journal 1893

But grow in the grace and knowledge of our Lord and
Savior Jesus Christ. —2 Peter 3:18

"*ALL THAT OUTWORKING OF HIS GRACE HAS COME SO SILENTLY.*" Lilias reflects,
as was her practice, on the anniversary of their first setting foot on North
African terrain: March 9, 1888. This year, however, was their thirty-fifth
anniversary, more than sufficient time to look back and observe significant
evidence of "expansion" in their ministry.

She reflects on the very nature of growth, noting that this is like God's work in *all* growth. Whether physical or spiritual, we don't see or hear growth happen! This is, perhaps, most obvious in the physical world. Periodic visits with our young grandchildren, even after only a few months' absence, invariably elicit the "my, how you've grown" response (no matter how we try to check that overworked welcome). A chart documenting their growth, age, and date verifies the same. But no one—present parents, absent grandparents—ever observed the very moments of growth. *Silently* . . . without observation.

Look at nature. Take a flower or a tree, for instance. Rarely (if ever) do we see or hear a flower open or a tree leaf out. But they do. *Silently* . . . without observation . . . season after season, year after year.

This past week was a return in time, in which this principle of growth was vividly witnessed. We attended a high school reunion, meeting schoolmates, some of whom we had not seen for half a century. (Name tags do help!) A reunion dinner concluded with reminiscences and current updates. Time had transformed untested teens—awkward, silly, wild, crazy, shy, earnest, driven— into full-blown adults, who have evolved, for the most part, into persons of depth, caring, and maturity. Growth: *silently* . . . without observation.

On an even more personal note, we took a sentimental journey back to the house of my youth, now boasting a stately pin oak tree, straight as an arrow, piercing the sky, great leafy branches shading much of the front lawn. This tree was the subject of much merriment when first planted. Based on careful research, my mother planted it with high hopes for its potential beauty and shade. Virtually a stick in the ground, it barely made it through the first season. Second season, she braced it with a pyramid of wire cords to correct a very definite bend. How we loved to tease Mother as we witnessed the seasons of struggle. But she held fast to her hopes. Now, decades later, we stopped the car, allowing me to pick up a fallen leaf to press in my journal. A reminder of the character of growth: *silently* . . . without observation.

The process of growth, by its very character, whether physical or spiritual, is contrary to what we by nature desire. We want results. Now. We want evidence that our efforts count. Society rewards and, for that matter, punishes by the same mentality. A losing season can cost a coach his job. An employee may be demoted or dismissed by failure to demonstrate results. The same mentality invades the ecclesiastical world: the number of people or programs—observable results (!)—becomes the measure of success.

So it is with our souls. We want results. Now. We resolve to do what it takes to become people of maturity. We read a chapter of Scripture, go to a Bible study or retreat, attend church, tackle a service project. It is so hard to measure the growth of a soul, but this we know: we often fall short of being the people we yearn to be.

Lilias concludes her reflections with a helpful insight on growth: "*All one can tell is that we have had nothing to do with its evolution except a measure of blind obedience—& oh that that measure had been fuller.*" Just as there are certain conditions that assure growth in the physical world—fertile soil, moisture, sun—there are conditions for growth in the world of the spirit. Our souls must be fed, yes, and we must be obedient to God's voice as we live out our lives of faith. For the most part it simply involves faithfulness to what we know we should do: asking, listening, obeying.

The transformation of the human heart, like all growth, is slow. It's a process by which, through time and intent, we develop the habit of divine orientation. We can no more identify each moment of our spirit's growth than we can the progress of a child to adult or a sapling to majestic tree. And yet, silently, without observation, our hearts are taking on a new character as we move quietly closer to God.

> How silently, how silently, the wondrous gift is given!
> So God imparts to human hearts the blessings of His heaven.
> —Phillips Brooks

Lord, reveal to me the growing points of my soul. Help me not to be stuck in the security of the past but to be open to change and growth.

The Roots of Spiritual Creation

Today's find was beautiful to the inward vision as well as to the outward. It was clusters of exquisite wild lilies—white and fragile and fragrant—growing out of the hot salt sand that drifts into dunes round the stunted juniper and lentisk bushes that fringe the shore. Down below the surface, the storage of reserve material in the lily bulbs had silently taken place . . . and there they had lain, shrouded and waiting. The hour had come now, and no adverse condition could keep back the upspringing. The same Lord over all can store the roots in His spiritual creation, even though they have but smothering sand drifts around them. —July 22, 1909; *Sand Lilies*

Painting: from booklet cover, *Sand Lilies*

For with you is the fountain of life. —Psalm 36:9

THE IMAGE OF SAND LILIES was one that touched the heart of Lilias not only aesthetically but spiritually. She marveled at the pristine blossom, "*white and fragile and fragrant,*" that managed somehow not only to survive the hostile desert but, in fact, to flourish: "*laughing to scorn the difficulties of their environment.*" Nourished by a hidden source of energy, "*their life was stored away, out of sight and there was enough for all the need.*"

She drew hope from this visual parable, hope that the spiritual dormancy she witnessed in a barren land would result, in God's timing, in a "*sudden miracle bloom out of these parched countries, and to show that He is 'King over all the earth.'*" The painting of sand lilies featured above was reproduced from the cover of a little booklet presenting both her belief in a day of dawning spiritually and a plea for prayers on behalf of that vision. Frequently the image of the "sand lily" would appear in her various writings circulated among fellow missionaries and partners in prayer.

The sand lily has taken on another meaning for me, first, in relation to Lilias who aptly was called Lily by her friends. Studying archives of her childhood, I witnessed the English Lily, nurtured in an ideal garden climate— rich, well-drained soil, moist air, sheltered site—the perfect environment for a pristine lily. All the natural resources—heredity, home environment, intellectual and artistic stimulation, spiritual nurture—would become "stored energy," spiritually speaking, requisite for survival in the harsh Algerian soil. The *Desert* Lily!

Then I consider the implications of this concept of "stored spiritual energy" for myself, for others. Scripture, on the one hand, speaks of a kind of "spiritual currency" that, in God's economy, is not stored in advance to draw upon at will but given directly by God, to meet the need of a given situation. On the other hand, not contradictory to that special dispensation of "grace" is the continual challenge of Scripture to be "rooted and built up" in Christ, "strengthened in the faith as you were taught" (Colossians 2:7). As with Lilias, certain factors contribute to the formation of our souls: heredity, environment, nurture, experiences good and difficult. Scripture continually challenges us to turn over all things—good and bad; past and present—to God for Him to work for our good . . . for the growth of our souls.

There is a strong parallel to physical training and spiritual formation. Just as a person builds strength and endurance through certain physical disciplines, we build a muscular faith by *spiritual* disciplines that sustain us daily and provide inner support in times of duress: meditation on Scripture, prayer, worship, service, fellowship with other believers. One could say that we are cultivating "stored energy" to be drawn upon in time of drought, when our soil is parched, no rain in sight. Desert lilies.

God has promised to be a "spring of living water" (Jeremiah 17:13). In turn, we "will be like a tree (lily!) planted by the water that sends out its roots by the stream." You or I can be the one who "has no worries in a year of drought and never fails to bear fruit" (Jeremiah 17:8).

❧ ❧ ❧

God, You are the spring of living water. May I intentionally drink from that water and be nourished by Your Word.

Soul Food

When Moses went in before the Lord to speak with Him, he took the veil off.
Bare absolute contact with God's Presence—if our times alone with Him were
but that all the time, they would be mighty in their outcome.

—August 16, 1901

Painting: from Pocket Sketchbook, France/Switzerland/Venice, 1877

Thy words were found, and I did eat them; and thy word was unto
me the joy and rejoicing of mine heart: for I am called by thy name,
O LORD God of hosts.   —Jeremiah 15:16 KJV

I LINGERED IN FRONT of the dessert table, studying the slices of cake arranged
on white plastic plates. I became aware that I was blocking a man behind me
and sheepishly admitted, "I was looking for the one with the most frosting."
He responded, "Take your time. I'm looking for the one with the *least* frosting."
Noting his trim physique, I ruefully acknowledged, "This, in microcosm, explains
a significant difference between the two of us."

Amy Carmichael, in her daily devotional *Whispers of His Power,* quotes an old English nursery rhyme:

> It's a very odd thing,
>   As odd as can be,
> That whatever she eats
>   Turns into Miss T.

She elaborates: "If we hastily read God's word, without taking the time to absorb it, we do not gain much. But if we take it into ourselves (Thy word was found and I did eat it), then it becomes part of us. It 'turns into Miss T.'"

"You are what you eat." How often have we heard that principle in relation to our physical well-being? It is just as applicable to the spiritual realm. We are profoundly affected by what we feed our souls. What better place to develop a basic, healthy menu than with a steady diet of Scripture: God's revealed Word. *Soul* food.

Lilias was keenly aware of needing "soul food" if she was to survive the challenges of her pioneer work in Algeria. Her yearly pattern allowed for a European break, including a fortnight "alone with God," frequently scheduled around family or ministry commitments. The exact site was often a matter of prayer and the "*little traces by which God leads us in the way of His steps,*" a story in itself.

Such was the case in September 1901, when she settled in an alpine village above Zermatt, in Switzerland. "*Up again tonight in a beloved Findelu—alone this time, & for a fortnight—such a gift from God for time with Him. It is looking lovelier than ever with the first tawny touches of autumn on the bilberry bushes.*" The driving force for her annual (and daily) retreats was one and the same: a soul hunger for God almost visceral in its intensity.

I searched her diaries and journals to discern a formula for her "times alone with God"—a Bible reading program, perhaps, or certain disciplines that would instruct my spiritual formation. To no avail. But I did discover some common elements to her "diet." For starters, I noted a ravishing hunger for God that led her to seek out places conducive to communion with Him, whether it be a quiet spot in a nearby woods or palm garden, a "place of prayer" in a rooftop room or desert outpost. There she drew a circle of quiet around her "bare soul" and waited for

God to speak, through His world, His Word, and through a collection of topically related Scriptures compiled in her well-worn leather volume, *Daily Light*. More often than not, God spoke first through His created order—daisy, dandelion, snow-diamond, firwood—which, in turn, connected her to Scripture: The peak of the Matterhorn "*linked on with that verse in Job.*" And, "*The thistles here are a commentary to me on that wonderful title of 1 Timothy 1:11, 'The Blissful God.'*" And the fog "*has been linking in, these days, with the 'forty days with God, of the Bible.'*" From there the conversation continues, she "*tracing in Scripture*" these lessons and/ or thoughts; she bringing them back to God for His instruction.

I am very much a novice when it comes to that kind of communion with God. But I believe it possible. And I do desire it. Prosaic soul that I am, I can't depend on my "beholdings" to lead me to the heights and depths of Lilias's experience; I have found value in a daily Bible reading schedule, particularly the Scripture Union Bible Reading Program, *Encounter with God*. It provides a plan that leads me in a systematic way through the Bible (Old Testament once and the New Testament twice every five years) guided by a brief commentary on each passage, written by a variety of trusted biblical scholars. Whitney Kuniholm, president of Scripture Union/USA, warns in a "Final Note" at the end of the current guide: "We must always remember that the point of the method is to meet God, to become more aware of him, to be in step with his Spirit. We learn the discipline because it puts us in a position to experience God."

Eugene Peterson, author of *Eat This Book*, sums this thought, describing the title phrase as "my metaphor of choice for focusing attention on what is involved in reading our Holy Scriptures formatively, that is, in a way that the Holy Spirit uses them to form Christ in us. We are not interested in knowing more but in becoming more ... This kind of reading ... enters our souls as food, enters our stomachs, spreads through our blood, and becomes holiness and love and wisdom."

Lord, increase my appetite for You. May I hunger for the soul food
that results in a healthy, resilient spiritual life.

Finishing Strong

It is a very solemn thing to realize that the physical, as well as the spiritual, life depends on that channel to the Upper Springs being kept clear for the quickening of the mortal body by the Spirit that dwelleth in us, till our work is done.

—Diary September 2, 1926

Painting: from Journal 1899

The righteous will flourish like a palm tree . . .
They will still bear fruit in old age, they will stay fresh and green.

—Psalm 92:12, 14

ALL SAINTS DAY, of the liturgical calendar, took on new meaning to me this year. Within two weeks, I said final good-byes to two women who have played significant roles in my life. The first good-bye was to a steadfast "saint" of the congregation my husband served for thirty-seven years. She was recognized in our church and community for her unflagging service sourced from her love of Jesus. I, like many others, was recipient of that unconditional love not only in acts of kindness but in a listening heart.

I had hardly put down the phone (or so it seemed) when I received another call, this time from my ancient past, informing me that a friend from my childhood was dying. Would I call and say "good-bye"? Once again, with trembly voice and teary eyes, I called this "saint" who so many years ago took a young child under her wings, building a library of hardback children's classics. She introduced me to Anne of Green Gables along with Heidi, Rebecca of Sunnybrook Farm, the Five Little Peppers, and Alcott's little women— wonderful "friends" who peopled my childhood. She took me on special excursions and filled the void in my homesick heart with letters when, at the age of ten, I moved with my family more than a thousand miles from my childhood home.

Through the lingering weepiness of the past several weeks, I ponder this loss. My loss. Not theirs. Both had lived long productive lives, well spent to the very end. Each eagerly anticipated "going Home." One wrote concerning her recent prognosis: "I am at complete peace. All my life I have worshiped and loved my Redeemer and Savior and now I will get to meet Him." They were ready to leave this earthly dwelling, their work done. They finished strong.

And that, perhaps, is my dominant takeaway: finishing strong. The same spirit of loving and serving and giving that characterized their active years sustained them to the end. They lived life to the full, at each stage, even as they accepted gracefully the inevitable losses of aging and illness. Friends and family gathered around their respective beds, during their last days, gave witness to being blessed by their presence—*to the end*. And this, to me, is their parting message: finish strong.

After retiring from his pastoral ministry, noted biblical commentator/ clergyman Charles Simeon (1759–1836) continued to get up at 4:00 a.m. each day to pray and study Scripture. When a friend suggested he could take it easier now, Simeon retorted, "Shall I not run with all my might when the winning post is in sight?"

Finishing strong. The psalmist proclaimed, "The righteous . . . will still bear fruit in old age, they will stay fresh and green." In his daily devotional on the Psalms, *The Songs of Jesus*, Tim Keller observes, "If we maintain fellowship with God over the years, there is a kind of 'freshness' that can come with increasing age. It is not the naiveté of perpetual spiritual adolescence. It is the spiritual vigor that grows only out of years of trusting God in prayer, coupled with the wisdom that comes from a treasure chest of rich memories, both sorrowful and sweet."

Our youngest son made an observation after visiting his ninety-five-year-old grandmother: "What an inspiring example of someone stretching and changing to meet the challenges of old age. It is a lesson to me: One never needs to stop growing at any age."

Lilias was a prime example of finishing strong. Confined to bed her last three years of life, she wrote *The Sevenfold Secret* for the Sufi mystics, arguably her magnum opus. Along with multiple projects, she wrote her love story with a people and the place of Algeria, illustrating *Between the Desert & the Sea*, with fifteen full-color plates of watercolors, subjects culled from her forty years of dairies and journals. Her daily log for 1927, her final full year, reveals a wide range of correspondence, personal and organizational, plans and projects for the future (without her), and the presence of individuals who peopled her life, staff and nationals. It is out of her very weakness that she wrote: "*It is a very solemn thing to realize that the physical, as well as the spiritual, life depends on that channel to the Upper Springs being kept clear for the quickening of the mortal body by the Spirit that dwells in us, till our work in done.*"

Finishing strong is not limited to one's final years. Indeed, I have been inspired by the individuals who have touched my life directly or indirectly through their stories. I note that each person ended as they lived. Their final parting was a culmination—a continuation—of a lifetime of a series of choices to finish strong whatever their occupation or vocation. Finishing strong was not a final flourish, a grand finish, to mark their final days. It was an MO for living all the ages and stages of their lives, all the actions and transactions of their days.

Once I was asked to fill in for a respected lawyer, to give a talk to adolescents on (of all things) the work place. Daunted by my task and short on script, I consulted him. "What counsel would you give?" One bit of advice remains with me to this day. "Whatever your present job, however humble—clerking at Wal-Mart; cooking at McDonald's—give it your best to the very end." He noted that the first recommendation your next prospective employer will seek is your last place of work. In other words: finish strong.

I'm saddened by the void left by these cherished friends and reminded that there will be others, beloved, who will leave this world before me. "Time like an ever-rolling stream bears all its sons (and daughters) away," says the hymn-writer. Yet my life has been enriched by both their presence and their example of how to live . . . and how to die.

Every day of every age and stage of life provides countless tasks and challenges to finish strong. But the fact is, we do tire. We become weary in well-doing. Over time we can become jaded by life itself, losing our early enthusiasm boosted by our ideals, our dreams. Discouraged by disappointments and setbacks, we wrap a protective blanket of cynicism around our hearts. Been there; done that. We can't seem to drum up the energy or enthusiasm to face our tasks and challenges much less finish strong.

This brings us to our true condition: dependent both physically and spiritually on the quickening of both body and soul by the "*Spirit that dwellest in us till our work is done.*" Today and each day till the end of our lives. No, we cannot always produce energy or vitality at will. But we can keep open "*the channel to the Upper Springs*"—that refreshment from God—as we nourish our souls through Scripture and prayer.

Lord, let me be connected to the Upper Springs that I may flourish and bear fruit. Refresh my body and soul with Your Spirit today and every day until my work is done. Amen.

Expect God to Triumph

Take the very hardest thing in your life—the place of difficulty, outward or inward, and expect God to triumph gloriously in that very spot. Just there He can bring your soul into blossom.   —*Parables of the Cross*

Setteth in pain
the jewel
of His
joy.

Painting: Color plate from *Parables of the Cross*

No discipline seems pleasant at the time, but painful, Later on,
however, it produces a harvest of righteousness and peace for those
who have been trained by it.   —Hebrews 12:11

THIS IS ONE of my favorite Lilias quotations. It rings with victorious affirmation.
It speaks to the deepest pain. I'm tempted to quote it verbatim and leave it alone.
I can't improve on the wording or, for that matter, on the content. While it can
rightly stand on its own, it does bear examination. What, really, does it mean?
More to the point, is it true? Does it have any practical bearing in my life today?

"*Take the hardest thing in your life . . . and expect God to triumph gloriously in that very spot.*" We all know stories of hardship and difficulty and how people have triumphed in spite of, or perhaps because of, that very difficulty. The periodic

Olympic events provide countless testimonials, showing a crowning achievement as the proportional result of hardship endured, difficulty overcome. No pain, no gain is also borne out in the spiritual realm. Difficulty endured produces something yet stronger. The greater the difficulty, the greater the triumph.

But there is a unique aspect to her claim that goes beyond the formulaic gain for pain. It is the promise of a triumph that transcends *our* efforts and resources to a work of *God* in the very place of our potential defeat. "*Expect God to triumph gloriously in that very spot.*" Not only will God bring triumph in the place of pain, but He will go beyond the particular need of the moment to the transformation of one's very soul: "*Just there He can bring your soul into blossom!*"

In her devotional classic *Parables of the Cross*, Lilias illuminates this truth with a parallel from nature. In delicate watercolors she paints a bit of gorse bush, branches bristling with thorns, large and small, stuck out in all directions. The thorns have been hardening and sharpening throughout the year, and even with the arrival of spring they do not drop off or soften. But halfway up the pictured thorn appears two brown furry balls, mere specks at first, that break at last, straight out of last year's thorn, into a blaze of golden glory!

Our difficulties, outward and inward, are like those thorns, unyielding and seemingly without relief. There is no apparent solution. No way out. No end in sight. They bring us to deep despair. We are dogged with questions: Where do we turn? How do we proceed? Sometimes there seems to be no good reason to go on.

It is here that the God of the gorse thorns looks down on us with love and says, "Do not despair. Nothing can happen to you that I cannot manage. Trust me." Elisabeth Elliot in *A Path through Suffering*, her reflection on this parable, writes,

> He wants to transform every form of human suffering into something glorious. He can redeem it. He can bring life out of death. Every event of our lives provides opportunity to learn the deepest lesson anyone can learn on earth . . . When our souls lie barren in a winter which seems hopeless and endless, God has not abandoned us. His work goes on. He asks our acceptance of the painful process and our trust that He will indeed give resurrection life.

I can look back over my life and see where pain was requisite for God's transforming work. I see evidence of this principle in the great heroes of the faith, biblical and more recent history. Then there are stories told to me that will never make the pages of history. But what about the here and now? Can I—can *we*—take the thorns that seem so unrelentingly hard and expect God to triumph in that very place? Fears for a loved one or for our own future . . . pain or disability that makes life unbearable . . . betrayal of a supposed friend or family member . . . injustice or misunderstanding in the workplace or no job at all . . . presence of a demanding person in our household . . . financial insecurity and limited resources . . . Can we believe that out of that very thorn will come a blossom fragrant and glorious? Can we trust that out of that difficulty God will bring our soul into blossom?

This quotation, illuminated by the simple gorse bush, presents the *problem*—difficulty, outward and inward; the *process*—take it to God with the expectation that *He* will triumph in that very place; and the *product*—a soul brought into glorious blossom!

> Blest be the Architect, whose art
> Could build so strong in a weak heart.
>
> —George Herbert

God, I bring to You the trials and tribulations of my life, trusting You to bring my "soul into blossom" at those very points of difficulty.

Part 5

Images of Prayer

Fire Upwards!

A story of the wars of the first Napoleon has often come back to me. He was trying in a winter campaign, to cut off the march of the enemy across a frozen lake. The gunners were told to fire on the ice and break it, but the cannon-balls glanced harmlessly along the surface. With one of the sudden flashes of genius he gave the word, "Fire upwards!" and the balls crashed down full weight, shattering the whole sheet into fragments, and the day was won. We can "fire upwards" in the battle, even if we are shut out from fighting it face to face.

—Challenge to Faith

Painting: from Sketchbook 1889

The LORD is near to all who call on him.   —Psalm 145:18

"PLEASE COME TO THE HOSPITAL. Max is in a coma," my friend urged. When Dave and I arrived at his bedside, everyone, even the attending doctors, seemed baffled. He had returned from a trip to Africa with a mild fever that they at first had "dismissed." But it lingered—and built—and while being treated at the hospital, he had taken a sharp turn for the worse. It was finally recognized as a form of malaria, but an unidentified strain that was unresponsive to standard treatment. We watched as his condition worsened, the attending doctor placing phone calls to centers of infectious disease even while poring over textbooks.

As plans were being made to transfer him to a larger medical center, we gathered around his bed, holding hands as we prayed, knowing that pressure was building in his brain and that time was running short—if it wasn't already "too late."

I returned home with a sense of desperation and helplessness. I placed a call to my mother (my own personal prayer warrior), asking her, and her friends, to pray. I dropped to my knees and begged God to spare our friend this grief. "It is too much," I told God, reminding Him that she previously had lost her young daughter and her first husband within the same year. And now this, her recently wed husband, Max. "It just can't happen," I pled. "Please heal Max."

Meanwhile, Dave arrived at church just as the weekly fellowship supper was to begin. Before opening the evening with grace, he reported the situation's urgency. Everything came to a halt while this family of faith fired-off their collective prayers. The very throne of God was bombarded during those few hours in which our friend's life was held in the balance. All we could do now was wait.

"We can 'fire upwards' in the battle, even if we are shut out from fighting it face to face." Lilias elaborated this prayer principle in the little leaflet she published titled *A Challenge to Faith*. She wrote in the context of, but not exclusive to, prayers for the unbelieving people she felt called to serve. The principle in any case is the same: the prayer of faith, on behalf of another, does not require us to be present bodily. In fact, we can be more completely present "*in the bright, free, spiritual air*" apart from the immediate battlefield than if we were present physically. The question she presents—the challenge of faith—is succinct: "*You may not have been definitely unbelieving, but have you been as definitely believing as the case demands?*"

Amy Carmichael, a contemporary of Lilias albeit serving in India, referred to this direct assault of heaven in prayer as "telegraph prayers." Today, perhaps, she would encourage "e-mails" or "texts" to God! But the idea is to pray—telegraph, text—the need of the moment directly to God, trusting Him for His answer.

A biblical precedent for this kind of prayer was set by Nehemiah, cupbearer to the king of Persia, on behalf of the remnant of the Hebrews in Jerusalem. For three months Nehemiah mourned, fasted, and prayed as he considered their plight and pondered his role in their deliverance. The moment finally came, when the king, noting Nehemiah's sadness, asked, "What is it you want?" One almost holds one's breath with Nehemiah as he prepares to make his request. But first he shot off an "arrow prayer" to God: "Then I prayed to the God of heaven" (Nehemiah 2:4), quietly, no doubt, but directly from his heart to the heart of God. We know the rest of the story. The king grants Nehemiah's request, freeing him for and aiding him in the rebuilding of the walls of Jerusalem!

Arrow prayers. Cannonballs. Telegraphs (or texts). Call them what you will, but they are, in essence, those prayers of our hearts shot directly to the heart of God. I suspect that many of us "shoot off" such prayers more times than can be counted. And, I believe, that God "hears" those prayers and understands the intensity of the moment and longings of our hearts. Perhaps He hopes, even designed, that our needs will throw us at His mercy and turn our hearts toward Him?

So what about Max? That was the question that the referring doctor asked the nurse several days later—assuming the worse. Her answer: "He is sitting up in bed watching a baseball game." After a stunned silence, the doctor replied, "I didn't think he'd make it. It is a miracle."

No one is too busy to *fire upwards*," sending our thoughts and desires of our hearts directly to the heart of God. As we continue this practice of prayer, throughout our daily rounds and common tasks, as well as in the times of crisis, we will be training our hearts ever God-ward even as we tune our hearts to His will.

Tune me O Lord, into one harmony
With Thee, one full responsive vibrant chord:
Unto Thy praise all love and melody,
Tune me, O Lord.

—Christina Rossetti

Vibrations

Each prayer-beat down here vibrates up to the very throne of God, and
does its work through that throne on the principalities and powers around
us . . . We can never tell which prayer will liberate the answer, but we can tell
that each one will do its work.

—From a "rough manuscript" adapted from her 1899 journal

Painting: from Journal 1899,
later adapted for a cover of the leaflet *Vibrations*

So I say to you: Ask and it will be given to you; seek and you will find;
knock and the door will be opened to you.

—Luke 11:9

IN HER DIARY Lilias records a strange occurrence. One of the pillars that
supported the gallery of their old Arab house had fallen down into the court
and lay shattered on the pavement, bringing in its wake a shower of bricks
and tiles from the arch above it. A consulting architect confirmed the probable
cause of the collapse. For six or seven years, a baker had occupied the adjoining
house. Every night, two men had swung on a see-saw that had kneaded their

bread; every blow backward and forward had vibrated through the house, until, at last, the *"result was seen in the shattering of masonry that had looked as if it would last as long as the world."*

She saw an object lesson from the physical world into the mysteries of the spiritual world: *"a truth, which had glimmered out before in thinking of the strange power of vibrations—once more 'the invisible things being understood by the things that are made.'"* She observed that there is a similar vibrating power in this world that can make its results evident in the invisible world.

> *Each prayer-beat down here vibrates up to the very throne of God, and does its work through that throne on the principalities and powers around us, just as each one of the repeated throbs from below told on the structure of our house though it was only the last one that produced the visible effect. We can never tell which prayer will liberate the answer but we can tell that each one will do its work.*

This concept she illustrates with two parables from the Gospel of Luke. The first is the parable of the man who appealed to another friend, in the middle of the night, to give him three loaves of bread because "a friend of mine on a journey has come to me, and I have no food to offer him" (Luke 11:6). The second is the plight of a widow who repeatedly appealed to a judge for justice (Luke 18). In both cases their plights were ignored and dismissed. The friend refused to answer the door due to the inconvenience of the hour; the judge dismissed the woman as of no interest to him. Both, finally, due to the persistence of their pleas, were granted their requests.

While each parable is distinct in content, both are rooted deeply in their culture. Hospitality being at the core of the Arab culture, it would have been common practice to borrow from a neighbor during a crisis of inadequate food supply—regardless of time of day (or night). A widowed woman would have been powerless in the legal system being, herself, marginalized in society.

The listeners would have related to these stories and understood the common denominators: (1) the helplessness of the people in question; (2) their refusal to give up asking; (3) the victorious results of the persistence. In short, the power of persistence. More to the point, given the context, the power of persistence *in prayer*.

Older versions of the Bible use the word *importunate*, assigning this the "prayer of importunity," and refer to these parables, in particular, as illustration of the same. I confess, I had to look up the meaning of *importunity* in the dictionary: "insistently and persistently." Lilias notes that while the lesson Jesus teaches in both parables is the same, their aims differ. The man at midnight represents those who ask on behalf of individuals coming to us asking for our help. Lilias suggests that the widow represents the person praying against the *"principalities and powers in heavenly places headed by the adversary the devil."*

I must admit, while I understand the principle of persistency, it seems fraught with problems. I can look back over my life (and witness the lives of others) and finger "answers"—the likely results of "persistent prayers." At the same time, all the while I identify "victories," my doubting-heart questions, what about this?; what about that? Various "failures" begin to leverage the scoreboard.

This is where I must move beyond subjective speculation to the objective teaching of Scripture. Jesus was intentional in His teaching about this particular aspect of prayer. He, in both instances, set up and followed up these story parables with a clearly stated purpose. The first was told in response to the disciples' request: "Teach us how to pray." The second was preceded by these words: "Then Jesus told his disciples a parable to show them that they should always pray and not give up" (Luke 18:1). He couldn't be clearer!

No, I don't understand how it works or at what point my prayers, solo or in concert with others, are the accumulative cause of a desired outcome. But this I know: Jesus told His disciples, replete with illustration, that they should always pray and never give up. And I can identify, even with my juvenile faith and myopic vision, certain things that happen when one does pray "insistently and persistently." Somehow prayers unite us in time and place with a host of "pray-ers" joined in common vision beyond the personal wants of one's own singular existence and, perhaps, even one's lifetime. We become collaborators with God's purposes as we subject our prayers to His will. Prayer does change things, we are told, and in the process it changes us.

So I will continue to let my prayer-beat join the sustained vibrations to the throne of God. Who knows which prayer will liberate the answer? At the end of the day, it is all about trust in our heavenly Father. Trusting His words; trusting His character.

Our son showed me a birthday letter written by his Daughter #4. As she has, perhaps more than her sisters, been anxious about an upcoming move that will remove her from the world of the familiar, this letter had special meaning. "Dad, you are the best dad ever! You always are there for me, and you are so encouraging. Whenever I am sad, you make me happy again. I guess you just have that magic touch. Even though I am sad about moving, *I know that if you are ready for this, I will be too* (my italics). I love you so much, and I hope your day has been great! Love, —"

Matthew gives a variation of Luke's account of Christ's concluding thoughts on prayer: "If you, then, though you are evil, know how to give good gifts to your children, how much more will your Father in heaven give good gifts to those who ask him!" (7:11).

So we ask . . . we seek . . . we knock. "Asking, seeking, and knocking does have an effect on God, as Jesus insists," writes Philip Yancey, in *Prayer: Does It Make Any Difference?*, "but it also has a lasting effect on the asker-seeker-knocker."

≫ ≫ ≫

O Lord, may I persist in seeking Your presence,
even as I trust You for Your answers.

Praying Scriptures

I have been praying the Lord's Prayer with special intention for Ali. It is such a wonderful vehicle for intercession if one puts it in the third person instead of in the first: "That the Father's name may be hallowed in him"

"That His Kingdom come and His will be done" "That he may have his daily bread and the Father's forgiveness" "That he may not be led into temptation but may be delivered from the evil one" "For in Him is the Kingdom and the power and the glory."

—Diary December 12, 1925

Pray in the Spirit on all occasion with all kinds of prayers and requests.

—Ephesians 6:18

Painting: from Pocket Sketchbook 1888

How DO WE PRAY when we don't know what to pray? Where do we begin? This was the dilemma Lilias faced as she worked day after day with Ali who, along with his brother, was assisting her in translating her Sufi book (*The Sevenfold Secret*) into the Arabic dialect distinctive to the people of Tozeur in the Southlands. They gathered at her bedside where she was confined even as she undertook, with their help, the tedious task of finding the best phrasing to make this work most accessible to them. As they labored together, they helping her with just the right thought or word (not "too deep" or "too heavy"), she saw this, likewise, as a unique opportunity to encourage and nurture these "sons of sunshine" in their fledgling faith.

Her heart was particularly heavy for Ali and the challenges he faced that seemed beyond her advisory ken. Then she seized upon the Lord's Prayer as a guide for her prayers on his behalf. After all, this was Jesus's answer to His disciples' request: "Teach us how to pray."

Prayer, by definition, is conversation with God. Yet it isn't always easy to get the conversation going, especially as we cannot look God in the eyes or see a response on a physical face. We hear no audible voice. Spirit-to-spirit communication requires a kind of concentration that does not necessarily come naturally. While many tools are suggested, if you will, to start the conversation, I often find them more conversation stoppers than starters. But if we agree that prayer is, indeed, a two-way conversation with God, what better way to start the conversation than with Scripture: God's words.

Praying the Scriptures. Lilias found praying the Lord's Prayer with intention for another to be a conversation starter, using it as a framework for prayer for others or for oneself. Others have suggested "praying the Psalms" noting the range of emotion and thought unleashed therein providing ample words of expression! Some have made a study of the prayers of the Bible (more than 650!), choosing prayers that express their particular concern or need.

One traditional approach to cultivating conversation with God, *lectio divina*, is the deliberate practice of "praying the Scriptures" in small portions, often from the gospel accounts of Christ. The idea is to take a short passage and read and meditate fully upon it, digest it, as it were, until one senses the very heart of that reading. Take that portion of Scripture that has touched you and turn it into prayer. Repeat this process, section by section, throughout the given passage of Scripture. The challenge is to be sensitive to how God's Spirit is guiding one's spirit into some new understanding or experience of His holy presence . . . to be open to any invitation from God to take action in a particular area of one's life.

For many years my attempts to set aside a time for communion with God was more an exercise in frustration or disappointment than a blessing. Then I read a chapter about meditation on Scripture in Paul Tournier's *Adventure in Living.* Since then I've become aware of many books with the same idea, but this is how it played out for me. With my Bible, daily/monthly planning calendar, notebook, and a cup of coffee, I settle in for a time of Bible reading. I ask questions about the reading: What is the main point? What do I learn about God? What insight am I given into myself or a life situation? What is required of me in response to this reading? Then I turn the things I have learned or wondered into related prayers of thanksgiving, confession, petition, or even, at its most transcendent, adoration. And, yes, I pray my doubts and questions. I pray Scripture. I pray thoughts prompted by listening to God's side of the conversation. He talks: I listen. I talk: He listens.

God has started the conversation. He has spoken through His Word and His world. So we listen. We speak. He listens. In His presence we can carry on a running dialogue with God, our Father and Creator.

A beautiful invitation is extended to us in Revelation 3:20: "Here I am! I stand at the door and knock. If anyone hears my voice and opens the door, I will come in and eat with him, and he with me." Listen. Open the door. Commune. *Communicate.*

Lord, so often I don't know how or what to pray. Help me to listen to You through Your Word and Your world that I might converse with You.

Why Pray?

It has come these days with a new light and power, that the first thing we have to see to, as we draw nearer to God day by day, is that "our fellowship is with the Father and with His Son Jesus Christ." If we can listen in stillness, till our hearts begin to vibrate to the thing that He is thinking and feeling about the matter in question, whether it concerns ourselves or others, we can from that moment begin praying downwards from His throne, instead of praying upwards towards Him. —Diary March 20, 1926

Painting: from Pocket Sketchbook 1878

Then Jesus told his disciples a parable to show them that they should always pray and not give up. —Luke 18:1

WHY PRAY? This week I have prayed about all manner of things. I've prayed sitting down, standing up, and moving forward in a car. I've prayed in faith, and I've prayed in doubt. I've prayed for the relatively trivial: my computer, that the "attachment" feature of my e-mail would work (still doesn't) and that the pop-up blocking function would disappear (it did, after five days!). I've prayed for the urgent: a health concern for my husband resulting in a night ambulance ride to the hospital (he's fine) and for my friend's ailing grandson (he's not fine). I've prayed down the list of friends and family; I've prayed for the tens of thousands suffering from a natural disaster. I've even thrown in a few Te Deums—prayers of thanksgiving—for good measure: whirl of a hummingbird hovering over a blossom; a passion flower in full and magnificent bloom.

Why pray? Does it make any difference? Were my "answers" to prayer really answers or the random working out of circumstances? And what about the "prayers" that seemed not to be answered? The problem of prayer, or rather the efficacy of prayer, is one that has dogged saints and sinners down through the ages.

The Bible is chock-full of prayers (see the Psalms). Jesus Himself prayed for His creatures and gave a model for praying (Matthew 6:9–13). From Augustine to the present day, books continue to be published exploring the mystery of prayer. (See Philip Yancey's *Prayer: Does It Make Any Difference?*— high on my list of a full and balanced treatment of the subject.)

Still the question continues to taunt both the trusting and the disappointed: *Why pray?* Does prayer really make a difference? Does God take into consideration my "requests" for myself, for others? Does He delight in my praise, infrequent as it may be?

A preschooler in the institute of prayer, I make my disclaimer: I don't have a thing to add to what has already been written, nor can I say it as well. But I continue to wrestle with the question. And I look to others further along in the understanding and practice of prayer.

I have been privileged to have witnessed, up close and personal, two veterans in prayer: my mother and her mother, my Grandma Bricker. I have a mental image of Mother seated in her bedroom chair, Bible open, praying quietly yet always available to the needs/wants of her family. I'm not sure *where* Grandma Bricker prayed, but if ever there was a need I knew I could appeal to both "prayer warriors," and they would lift their hearts and prayers to God at the very moment of the need in question.

A favorite account, now family legend, occurred when I was in junior high, vacationing at a lake house with my cousin. A mouse scurried under the bed. Silly girls, we hopped up on the bed and screamed for help. Grandma responded. (Where were the others?!) Soon Grandma reappeared, this time with a wastebasket in one hand and a broom in the other. Moving across the room, with her brisk, stiff-legged walk, she murmured all the while: "Lord, we have a mouse to kill. Lord, we have a mouse to kill." We'll never know whether the demise of the mouse was attributable to her prayers. But this we do know: she was walking each arthritic step with Jesus!

Lilias's journals would make a wonderful study of a *life* of prayer. Reading chronologically, one observes her exploration of different kinds of prayers for specific situations. There were incidents of her throwing herself on God's mercy for direction, of putting God to the test for a "proving" of His power, for bombarding the very heavens with the collective strength of many, for "going it alone—with God" for want of the presence of others.

There was also a definite shift in her approach to God as indicated in her journal entry, March 20, 1926, cited above. She is suggesting, in essence, that if we develop the habit of listening to God, we can begin to pray *His* thoughts! His thoughts will vibrate with our thoughts, making clear His will; in turn, we can pray with confidence that those prayers will be answered, being, after all, God's thoughts.

I note that another person of prayer, C. S. Lewis, observed that some saints with special gifts and unusual closeness to the Lord supernaturally discern that they are to ask God for what He has purposed, concluding that such prayers are "for very advanced pupils indeed," admitting that he did not consider himself one of those "advanced pupils."

It comforts me that the likes of Lewis, whom I consider a "postdoctoral student" of prayer, admits his "limitations," and that Lilias herself continued to be a "student of prayer" to the end of her life, delighting in and giving out E. Herman's *Creative Prayer* for its insights.

Why pray? I've raised the question, and now I will suggest, in brief, several elementary reasons to pray:

> 1. **Out of obedience.** We are commanded to pray. This reoccurring theme runs through the Old and New Testaments.

2. Because Jesus prayed. Repeatedly the Gospels show Jesus seeking out time to be with His heavenly Father. They record more than a dozen specific prayers by Jesus, along with several parables and teachings on the subject.

3. Because we really, at the end of the day, just can't help it. People from all time who did not even recognize deity turned to God in times of need or created their own gods to satisfy that appetite. As Emilie Griffin noted in *Doors into Prayer*, "The need to pray is primitive and fundamental."

What happens when we pray is the stuff of yet another conversation. But for now, I conclude my musings with words from two well-known sources. Elisabeth Elliot wrote, "Pray when you don't feel like praying. Pray till you *do* feel like praying." Or, in the words of Nike, "Just do it!"

Pray.

Father, who am I to question "why pray?" when Jesus constantly sought Your presence through prayer? Help me to desire the Giver more than the gifts and rest in communion with You.

Standing in Spirit

"Prayer is to us the opening of the sluice-gate between my soul and the Infinite."
I came on those words of Tennyson's the other day, and they came back again
and again today with a special sense of the reality with which, instantly and
unfailingly the taking in the Name of Jesus for this and that village and for
all those dear unreached and unreachable mountains and deserts does set the
sluicegates open to them. The powerlessness to go gives an intensity to the joy of it.

One can stand in spirit among the dear mud-huts of Tolga, and the
domed roofs of the Souf and the horseshoe arches of Touzer and tiled huts buried
in prickly-pear hedges in the hills, and bring down the working of the Holy
Ghost—by faith in that Name—perhaps more effectually than if one were there
bodily. One can "shut the door," as it were, and stand alone with God over it, as
one cannot do on the spot, with the thronging outward distractions of the visible.

—Diary March 26, 1904

Painting: watercolor from her Journal, "A Week in a Strong City" 1908

We live by faith, not sight.   —2 Corinthians 5:7

WE HAVE JUST RETURNED from a brief visit to Lake Wales—home of
our hearts for almost four decades. There I luxuriated in fellowship at a
church-family dinner; spoke to our MOPS group, fresh-faced mothers of

preschoolers, eagerly armed with loving ideals; attended the monthly meeting of my Circle Sisters. We savored each and every moment with dear ones— friendships forged over the decades of ups and downs of everyday living.

On the way out of town, we made one brief and final visit with our own "personal prayer warrior" (albeit not exclusively to us alone!). When we arrived in Lake Wales, callow kids, not yet thirty years old, she was at her peak of strength and involvement. An educator—public and Sunday school—her life was characterized by service. Now her activities are limited to the reach of her increasingly limited strength. As we listened to her testimony of gratitude for God's grace, we witnessed a spirit no less vital or relevant than the vigorous soul of forty years past. And, I confess, I slipped her a picture of our family, twenty-one strong, knowing that she will continue to pray for them by name. As she does for others.

"*One can stand in spirit . . . perhaps more effectually than if one were there bodily.*" When Lilias wrote these words, more than a hundred years ago, she was referring to people and places scattered over the face of Algeria that she had neither the time nor energy to visit personally, many with whom she had forged relations, individuals who indicated a spirit hunger for God. How her heart ached for contact with those people, to look them in their eyes, to assure and be assured of their well-being, spiritually, as well as in other aspects of their lives. Reassured not only by the spirit connection between her soul and God, she had the additional insight of the potential of concentrated power of prayer, free from "*the thronging outward distractions of the visible.*"

What a wonderful concept: *standing in spirit* for our loved ones! The thought that my prayers may even be more effectual by my absence than by my presence—"*without distractions*"—is comforting to me, separated by miles, from family and friends of many decades.

I have been blessed to have had people who "stood in spirit" for me all my life: Grandma Bricker from her Michigan farm, my parents after I left home, a church with individuals who embraced a young minister (and his even younger wife) and "stood in spirit" as we learned on the job how to shepherd a flock while raising a family—many of whom continue to "stand in spirit" for us as we begin a new chapter of life "off-site."

Just as we have been covered with prayer, it is a comfort to know that we, in turn, can "stand in spirit" for our loved ones, out of sight but not out of mind. We long to "be there" for our adult children, to be able to "do for" our grandchildren—to embrace them in our arms—but, in truth, we can "stand in spirit" for them, embracing them in our hearts, keeping up with their needs and concerns and translating them into prayers on their behalf. We can "stand in spirit" with ministries, those who implement them, those who benefit from them. And, yes, even now when it seems our country suffers from divisiveness and diversity, we can "stand in spirit" for those who lead and for those who are led.

I conclude, with Lilias, and with the countless people of prayer who have gone before her and have followed after her: "*the powerlessness to go*"—to "*be there on the spot*"—need not inhibit the power of God to hear and to respond, with His infinite wisdom, to the prayers of our hearts.

"Prayer is to us the opening of the sluice-gate between my soul and the Infinite."

Lord, You know how helpless I feel when separated from hurting loved ones. I "stand in spirit" on their behalf, knowing that You hear my prayers and that You are present to them.

Prayer Disappointments

The Noria in the garden has taught a prayer-lesson today. At the very first turn of the wheel that works it, a cupful of the clear cold water deep down is dipped up—but it does not reach the surface at once. Many and many a "godet" comes up first—dry, empty, iron. It is all

The Well in the Orchard.

Painting: from Diary July 1906

on the way to the full one that is coming. More than that, each disappointing godet that looks as if it might be the expected one and fails to be, and goes back as it came, means another full cup coming up, if only we go on turning. For once the first has risen brimming over, every fresh turn means another and another outpour. The prayer-disappointments are all part of the prayer-answers that are coming— linked as securely as the godet links of the Noria, and working out the one objective.   —Diary July 26, 1906

Do not be anxious about anything, but in everything, by prayer and petition, with thanksgiving, present your requests to God.
—Philippians 4:6

OUR COMMUNITY OF FAITH SUFFERED, with the parents, the loss of their son. We had prayed and rejoiced along with the family for successful treatment of his addiction only to see his young life taken unexpectedly— and accidentally—by a small but lethal combination of alcohol and a single nonprescription pill. My friend, the bereaved mother, related her struggle to make sense of things even as she tried to cope with staggering loss. "People ask me, has this made you lose your faith in God? And I answer, 'No, I'm not angry with God, but I am disappointed.'"

Disappointed in prayer. Who of us has not, at some time, felt the same way? We have prayed and prayed, and it seems our prayers were not heard or, at least, not answered. What do we do with our "prayer-disappointments" or what seems to be God's failure to answer our prayers? The common answer to that perplexity is, He *does* answer. But the answer may be no or later.

But what if "later" is "too late," as in the case of this heartbroken family? We can think of countless other instances of fervent prayers where there was no "later." I think of my mother with tears in her eyes, recalling a half century later, the death of her little brother to tetanus, just months before the discovery of the miracle drug that could have cured him. Too late.

And that doesn't even address the millions of lives lost in senseless wars, persecutions, or natural disasters. If God does not "answer" the earnest pleas that have been prayed on behalf of the suffering masses, how can we expect Him to attend to our singular concerns? What is the point of praying for health, children, safety, finances, particular ministries or individuals?

Lilias addresses prayer disappointments through a lesson taught by a garden noria, a waterwheel with attached buckets used to raise water from a stream or well. She observed how each time the wheel was turned, the *godet*—iron bucket—came up empty. Yet at the bottom of the well, the godets were being filled with clear, cold water. Every bucket that came up empty brought them closer to the desired water "*if only we go on turning.*" Comparing it to the spiritual world, she writes: "*The prayer-disappointments are all part of the prayer-answers that are coming—linked as securely as the godet links of the Noria, and working out the one objective.*"

The lesson, once again, is to persist in prayer, even when there seems to be no answer—at least the one(s) we crave. To keep on praying until our prayers are answered or until our prayers seem to make sense of things—from God's point of view. The very persistence of praying seems to have its own unique benefit even if I cannot see it now or, for that matter, ever.

Question: Is this spiritual gobbledygook? Why do we, why *should* we, continue to pray even when each godet comes up empty? Is it wishful thinking to believe that all the prayers that seem to no avail actually are working toward the inevitable and endless pull of water-filled buckets of answered prayer?

I could skirt the question with an answer that is straight from Scripture and, I believe, true in its essential understanding. Why pray? Because we are commanded to pray, to bring every need or thought to God in prayer. If that is not enough reason, we have the example of Jesus—God-incarnate—living out a life of prayer: mostly for others but for Himself as well (especially as He faced His last hours on earth). He could have brought immediate healing or help to any need that presented itself. He could have called upon all the powers of heaven to deliver Him from the hell into which He would descend.

One of my ways of coming to terms with the death of my mother was to read her journals, at least the ones that survived "the purge." With the turning of each page, I read the "inside story" of her faith experience, which elicited questions of my own. She claimed, in faith, promises of Scripture as she held before God the deepest concerns of her heart. Even as I "heard" her heartfelt prayers, I knew the outcome. And I knew that regardless of the nobility of her prayers and/or the purity of her motive—to bring glory to God—that certain prayers would not be answered in the way she believed would do so. And I ached for her even as I anticipated what she did not: prayer disappointments.

What I don't know is how, in her inner being, she came to terms with the same. Her journals "go dark" for almost a decade. But this I know: she came out of the darkness of disappointment with a faith in God that was vibrant and rock solid. The faithfulness of God would be both her unyielding testimony and legacy. Yes, through her prayers and life, she did demonstrate that for which she prayed: to bring glory to God.

I look at my own inner history of prayer: the prayer answers along with the prayer disappointments. And I wonder, if the godet came up full each time, what would I have gained? Trust in a Santa-on-steroids, there to do my beck and call? If each godet came up full, would I have tipped my hat to

God, saying, "thank you very much," and moved on? What would I have lost? Is it possible that turning to God with my needs, my questions, my doubts, I was actually coming closer to His intention for me? To depend on Him? To trust Him?

Certainly there were situations in which I would have liked a different answer. I could justify how it would work for the good of all. But there are many more prayers—prayer disappointments—that God worked out in ways vastly superior to my imaginings.

Can I trust that what He has done so lovingly in the past He will continue to do in the future? Even a future of which I may not be present? Can it be that every "empty" godet has brought me closer to Him? Has forced me to come to a greater understanding of His will and His ways? Has made me desire the Giver even more than His gifts? Could it be that ultimately this is what prayer is all about: grappling with the difficulties of living in this broken world, yes, but in collaboration with God and His purposes?

Karl Barth, living in the crisis days of Nazi rule, declared prayer "to be the true and proper work of the Christian." In *Creative Prayer*, E. Herman wrote, "Prayer is the soul's pilgrimage from self to God." What we perceive as prayer disappointments and/or prayer answers are a part of that pilgrimage. So we keep turning the wheel, so to speak, trusting that whatever is, or is not, in the godet is an essential aspect in that pilgrimage: the pathway to God.

Lord, sometimes it feels like my prayers make no difference at all.
Help me to trust You even when there seems to be no answer.

Is Not Jesus Enough?

The thought of Christ's intercession has taken on a new preciousness these last days. I was reading how God had given a wonderful gift of prayer to two friends. They would fight through together till His

answer came over in showers. And the thought came—oh that we had someone among us here able to pray like that. Then with the vividness of an audible voice almost, the thought came: "Is not Jesus enough?" Since then the sense of praying with Him alongside has been so beautiful.
—Diary March 23, 1904

... because [Jesus] always lives to intercede for them.
—Hebrews 7:25

Painting: from 1899 Diary

OH, THAT I HAD SOMEONE ... How many times, through my childhood and youth (adulthood!) has this thought passed through my mind. Someone who completely understands me (translated: "agrees with me"), someone immediately accessible to respond, at my whim, to my each and every mood. Perhaps this "perfect-friend-seed" was planted during my childhood obsession with the *Anne of Green Gables* books and her search for and conquest of a "kindred spirit."

Truth is, with increased life experience we come to understand that we cannot—should not—look to any one person to meet all our needs. It is a false expectation. It just isn't possible. So we try to patch together a support system to carry us through the roller coaster of emotions from the tedium of everyday routines to the joyous ecstasy of occasional highs, seeking to balance relational supports with the constructs and activities that uplift and sustain the spirit.

But sometimes we hit a brick wall. It could be situational: a move, a new baby, change in vocation. It could be trauma: death, disaster, divorce. It could be an acute but temporary crisis: faced and fixed. Or it could be a chronic situation without any real end in sight. And with such challenges comes an overwhelming sense of despair. Even surrounded with people, we feel an inner isolation. Loneliness. Whom can I trust? To whom can I turn? Is there "a safe place"? Vulnerable to "fill the void," we turn to a quick fix which, in the end, serves as salt to an unquenchable thirst.

While much of Lilias's writing focuses on God-affirming, life-affirming observations, sometimes weariness and isolation seep into her journals: references to a heavy heart, sleepless nights, skies of brass blocking her prayers. As indicated in the above diary entry, she longed for a friend who would partner alongside her in the "*wonderful gift of prayer.*" Someone who fully understood her mission. Someone who could be counted on to call forth the very gates of heaven on behalf of her vision. Then, into the stillness, spoke a thought almost audible in its clarity and affirmation: "*Is not Jesus enough?*"

There have been times in my life when my carefully constructed emotional/spiritual scaffolding has failed me. My support system has not been equal to my need: a childhood move . . . a college breakup . . . crisis in ministry . . . a block in parenting . . . a relational disappointment . . . hidden health concern . . . a major life transition . . . At such times I'm overcome with an acute sense of aloneness, even hopelessness. What do I do? Where do I turn? And the question is apt: *Is not Jesus enough?*

As long as my support systems worked, I was content to lean on others. It was only when they didn't that—yes, I confess, as last resort—I turned solely to Jesus and sought from Him what He offered all along: to come alongside me . . . to pray to the Father on my behalf . . . to be my sufficiency.

Richard Foster, in his small volume *Sanctuary of the Soul*, relates a particular crisis in his life that led to self-pity and frustration.

> My walking took me into a nearby woods and, as I walked along by the light of the moon, my complaining prayers began to diminish and I became more and more quiet. Finally, I fell into total silence. A still listening silence. It was then that God spoke, spoke out of the stillness and into my frustration . . . "You are frustrated and sorry for yourself," God seemed to be saying. "Sorry for yourself because you do not have all your desires satisfied. But if you will be *with me* you do not have to have all your desires satisfied. *With me* is ultimate and complete satisfaction. If you are genuinely *with me* you are in the best place possible."

He acknowledged that while nothing outwardly changed at the moment—nor was there any assurances of the same—*he* changed. "The voice of the true Shepherd was altogether sufficient."

"*Is not Jesus enough?*" At the end of the day, He is the only sure thing. "My grace is sufficient for you" (2 Corinthians 12:9). He promises. Can we appropriate the same?

Lord, You have promised to intercede on my behalf. Speak the prayers for which I have no words.

A Place to Escape Unseen

The days have seen the completing of another of the longings that have been brooding with its stress on the need of making Mission Houses to be houses of prayer, not just centers of activity. The longing had shaped itself into the need for a prayer-room, where those who felt the need of being quietly with God, alone or together, could escape unseen. We had debated the matter several times as to where in this big network of rooms such a place could be found and my solution did not find much backing, for though acknowledged to be quiet and hidden, it was considered dark and chilly and airless—being the old Moorish bathroom of former days, and a little vaulted chamber on a back stair. But now that the window opening is cleared out and all is whitewashed and its seats cushioned in green cotton, it is perfectly delightful. —Diary April 8, 1925

Painting: from Journal 1893

Yet at present we do not see everything subject to him.
But we see Jesus. —Hebrews 2:8

C. S. Lewis, in an article for the *Atlantic Monthly*, "The Efficacy of Prayer," relates an incident in which he was about to put off a haircut, the result of a change in other plans. Then an "almost unaccountable little nagging in my mind, almost like a voice saying, 'Get it cut all the same. Go and get it cut,'" overruled his decision, and he went anyway. It turns out that his barber had been praying that Lewis might come that day, having run into troubles for which he wished to consult him. "And in fact if I had come a day or so later I should have been of no use to him."

Lewis goes on to ponder prayer. Awed as he was by this experience, he recognized that one cannot rigorously prove a causal connection between the barber's prayers and his visit. Some might say it was telepathy. Others an accident. A coincidence. He goes on to raise the question that many have asked before as well as after him, "What sort of evidence *would* prove the efficacy of prayer?" And then he addresses the mystery of prayer: "The thing we pray for may happen, but how can you ever know it was not going to happen anyway?"

Prayer. Do our prayers really matter? For every instance of answered prayer, how many others seem to have hit ceilings of brass? There have been countless studies and surveys on prayer—in both secular and sacred worlds—efforts to weigh or measure the "effects" of prayer. Interesting statistics emerge. It appears that every "faith" has some form of prayer. Even so-called atheists find ways to pray. (It seems that the old adage "There are no atheists in foxholes" holds true under pressure.) Prayer seems to speak to some basic need in us. According to a recent Gallup poll, more Americans will pray this week than exercise, drive a car, have sex, or go to work. Nine out of ten pray regularly. Three out of four claim to pray every day.

Yet having said that, most people (myself included) are not satisfied with the time spent in prayer. Philip Yancey, in researching for his book *Prayer: Does It Make Any Difference?*, had his publishers conduct a website poll and, "of the 678 respondents only 23 felt satisfied with the time they were spending in prayer."

Lilias never wrote a comprehensive treatise about prayer, yet her diaries are a virtual chronicle of her pilgrimage of prayer: placing the needs of each moment—external plans, internal attitudes—before God for His input and guidance. For her, prayer, in its essence, was communion with God. Leaning over her shoulder, so to speak, peering into her diaries (like a voyeur), I was eyewitness of her journey of faith. Regularly, she recorded "faith lessons" as she explored the mysteries of prayer. Some she printed in little leaflets for the benefit of others. Although there appeared to be certain kinds of prayers for certain types of situations, there also seemed to be, through the years, an evolution in her understanding of prayer.

After more than three decades in Algeria, she was still exploring ways in which to make prayer more central to her life and to those who worked alongside her. Inspired by "the trip of a lifetime" to Jerusalem, she returned to Algiers determined to bring an intention into reality: "*a prayer-room, where those who felt the need of being quietly with God, alone or together, could escape unseen.*" Having created, at last, the perfect place, she "*put a text round the plinth from which the groining of the arches sprung. 'We see not yet all things put under Him—but we see Jesus.' May that vision abide there and the prayer of faith will arise and triumph.*"

Whether the din of the Casbah or the dust of the desert, little matter. What is important for any Christian seeking intimacy with God is to find that space, virtual or physical, to "*escape unseen*" into His Presence.

God, there is so much about prayer that I don't understand, and yet You instruct me to pray. Help me, in spite of my questions, to seek that quiet place to fellowship with You.

Part 6

Images of Service

A Flower That Stops
at Its Flowering

*A flower that stops short at its flowering misses its purpose. We were created
for more than our own spiritual development; reproduction, not mere
development, is the goal of matured being—reproduction in other lives.*

—*Parables of the Cross*

Painting: from Travel Journal 1900

And we pray this in order that you may live a life worthy of the Lord
and may please him in every way: bearing fruit in every good work,
growing in the knowledge of God, being strengthened with all
power according to his glorious might.   —Colossians 1:10–11

BLUE BUTTERFLY PLANT.* My most recent discovery and, modestly speaking,
horticultural success. Little matter that once rooted it is almost impossible to
destroy. Its true blue flowers have an uncanny resemblance to butterflies in
flight—their delicate stamens arching upward like intricate antenna.

I netted a branch with several "butterflies" aloft and placed it in a bottle-

Clerodendrum ugandense (botanical name for blue butterfly plant)

green vase to study and savor. Somewhere between branch and bottle, the seam of the bud sepal split open, revealing a hint of blue within. Suddenly I became possessed of a plan to watch the bud unfold before me. To "catch it," so to speak, as it was opening. Although I had seen a bud unfurl in a time-exposure nature film, I'd never seen the moment of opening in real time. Surely this bud was ripe and ready. And I was determined to see it happen! (Oh, the joys of retirement!)

So I watched and watched. And watched. Nothing happened. Well, it *had* to happen, didn't it? At some point in time, the seams would split and the bloom would appear. I was more determined than ever to be witness to the moment. I moved the vase next to the computer where I could multitask: write a letter; keep a sharp eye on the bud.

I had hardly turned my head to start up the computer when it happened—the grand opening—in the split second I averted my gaze. But the show continued: I watched as the wandlike filaments ever so gradually unfurled into a crescent-shaped arch. Much like a midwife, I felt, watching (if not aiding) the birthing of a new life. I carried the vase with the newborn "butterfly" with me from desk to dinner table to bedside glorying in its flawless beauty.

I was eager to check it out the next day. Would a new bud bloom? (Just how much time did I have?!) Much to my disappointment, my beautiful butterfly bloom had withered and died. Whether William Blake had his own literal butterfly experience—winged insect or flower—we may never know, but his poem "Eternity" captures the ephemeral nature of beauty:

> He who binds to himself a joy
> Does the winged life destroy;
> But he who kisses the joy as it flies
> Lives in Eternity's sunrise.

Lilias has her own "take" on the transitory life of a flower—and my lament. The flower stage of a plant's life is, for all its beauty, only a passing stage in the purpose of the plant. "*A flower that stops short at its flowering misses its purpose.*" She notes the high cultivation of flowers that spends its whole energy on the production of bloom at the expense of seed: "*The flowers that are bent on perfecting themselves, by becoming double, end in barrenness.*"

She proceeds to the inevitable parallel in the life of the soul and a like barrenness that "*comes to the soul whose interests are all concentrated upon its own spiritual well-being, heedless of the needs around.*"

Clearly there is a tension here, between attending to our own personal spiritual development and slipping into an obsessive self-focus that results, potentially, in a useless hybrid. I was raised in a family, and faith culture, with a strong sense of "holiness" and striving for the perfecting of character. This was supported and augmented with a set of standards to ensure (or at least encourage) the same. As an adult this evolved into an internal sense of morality and a heart desire to honor God. Toward that end, I strived to be a particular kind of person who would bring glory to God. But *strive* was the operative word, and, needless to say, I fell hopelessly short of my goal!

Imagine my surprise when I came across words penned by one of my favorite authors, Paul Tournier: "In this world our task is not so much to avoid mistakes as to be fruitful." How easy it was, in my efforts for self-improvement, to miss the point! And what a relief to increasingly take the focus off of myself as I began to form a clearer sense of God's design for His children: "*We were created for more than our own spiritual development; reproduction, not mere development, is the goal of matured being—reproduction in other lives.*"

As to the matter of "holiness," in *A Path through Suffering*, Elisabeth Elliot brings liberating perspective:

> We cannot make ourselves holy. But when we surrender ourselves to the Lord, learning day by day to treat all that comes to us with peace of soul and firm conviction that His will governs all, He will see to our growth in grace. He will so govern the events in our lives, down to the smallest detail, as to provide for us the conditions that may make us fruitful. It is not for our sake but for the sake of others.

I will savor my blue butterfly blossoms, and countless other flowers that bloom and die, as lovely reminders of an important spiritual truth: "*The true, ideal flower is the one that uses its gifts as means to an end; the brightness and sweetness are not for its own glory; they are but to attract the bees and butterflies that will fertilize and make it fruitful. All may go when the work is done—'It is more blessed to give than to receive.'*"

God, forgive my self-absorption.
Help me to be fruitful in service to You through serving others.

Vocation of Loving

I have been thinking lately what a work for God it is, just loving people.
He says in Deuteronomy 22, "If an ox or an ass has gone astray, thou
shalt bring it unto thine own house, and it shall be with thee till thy
brother seek after it." I think He gives us sometimes a like service for
souls—wandering souls that we cannot bring back to Him. Sometimes all
we can do is to keep them near us, and show the kindness of God to them,
and hold them in faith and prayer till He comes to seek them.

—Journal April 25, 1891

Painting: undated

We love because he first loved us. —1 John 4:19

A VOCATION OF LOVING. Can loving truly be considered a vocation? This
was the question Lilias pondered early on in her ministry to Algiers. The above
diary entry was written in relation to her decision to focus her team's limited
resources of time and energy on the Arab people in the Casbah, a critical
decision that would inevitably limit her work with other people. She found

solace in believing that there was a *"service for souls"* even in simply holding them close through faith and prayer.

If ever there was a vocation of simply "loving," Lilias was its personification. Her vocation of loving did not begin in North Africa. It began when, as a young woman of considerable means and exceptional talent, she reached beyond the volunteerism popular with her peers. She ministered not only to the hapless prostitutes at Victoria Station, but also helped them break from that lifestyle by setting up shelters and programs that gave them entrée to self-supporting respectable jobs. At the same time, recognizing the spiritual poverty of women of means, she offered "at homes" in her upscale residence in London, providing opportunity to study the Bible. And for working-class women, forced to eat bag lunches on the London sidewalks, she established the first public restaurants for women.

She intended to spend her life "loving London" until an encounter with God led her to leave the comforts of home and family and venture to North Africa. Her call was to bring the "light and life and love" of Jesus to people who had never heard His name. It should come as no surprise that love compelled her to move into the Casbah, the old city of Algiers, to come alongside the women and children who were love starved, having left the harems of their fathers to enter, at the age of twelve, those of their husbands, only to be cast off, eventually, for yet younger brides. Her love eventually went beyond the old city to mountain villages and then deep into the desert, where she brought the love of Christ to the searching Sufi mystics of the Southlands.

It is tempting, at face, to look at Lilias and conclude that this is not the life for me, that my love falls short. Nonetheless, a "vocation of loving" is not really an option for any person who claims to be a follower of Christ. Loving was mandated in Scripture in response to the question, "What must I do to inherit eternal life?" Jesus answered, "'Love the Lord your God with all your heart and with all your soul and with all your strength and with all your mind'; and, 'Love your neighbor as yourself'" (Luke 10:27). He followed up with the parable of the Good Samaritan to further define one's "neighbor" as the wounded stranger. In so doing, Christ settled once and for all the indiscriminate nature of love. By laying down His life, Christ demonstrated the ultimate measure of love: "This is love: not that we loved God, but that he loved us and sent his Son as an atoning sacrifice for our sins. Dear friends, since God so loved us, we also ought to love one another" (1 John 4:10–11).

Mother Teresa wrote, "Not all of us can do great things. But we can do small things with great love." Love begins in our homes in the smallest courtesies (to the smallest person) and extends beyond those walls to our neighborhood, our church, our community. Love continues, potentially, through every interaction throughout each day—at school, workplace, playground, shop, post office—in every place we travel, to every person we greet. I am not Mother Teresa (or Lilias Trotter, for that matter), but I can love. And when love is too much for me to muster, God can love through me.

Love knows no boundaries. In *The Hiding Place*, Corrie ten Boom wrote, "I made another discovery about love. Mama's love had always been the kind that acted itself out with soup bowl and sewing basket. But now that these things were taken away, the love seemed as whole as before. She sat at her chair at the window and loved us. Her love took in the city, the land of Holland, the world. And so I learned that love is larger than the walls that shut it in."

Lilias, the active pioneer, spent the last several years of her life in bed. Behind her hung a map of North Africa. Daily she prayed through each mission station—people and ministries—along the coast and down into the desert. She penned letters, itemized by name and topic in her daily log; she wrote and painted. She never stopped reaching out in love. Her contribution to the world may never be accurately measured. But she lived a vocation of love. She left a legacy of love.

London; Algeria; Holland; Mt. Dora, Florida. Little matter. Love.

Lord, You have touched my heart with Your love.
Let me love others with the love You have given me.

Radiating Every Ray

We ourselves are "saved to save"—we are made to give—to let everything go if only we may have more to give. The pebble takes in all the rays of light that fall on it, but the diamond flashes them out again: every little facet is a means, not simply of drinking more, but of giving more out. The unearthly loveliness of the opal arises from the same process carried on within the stone: the microscope shows it to be shattered through and through with numberless fissures that catch and refract and radiate every ray that they can seize. —Parables of the Cross

Painting: from Diary 1908

The Lord Jesus himself said: "It is more blessed to give
than to receive." —Acts 20:35

"WE ARE MADE TO GIVE." This is a life-giving principle. Scripture couldn't be clearer. Jesus said, "Give, and it will be given to you." And then, just in case we didn't get the message, He elaborated: "A good measure, pressed down, shaken together and running over, will be poured into your lap" (Luke 6:38).

If that were an exact economic equation—give a certain amount of

money and get back a certain percentage more in return—that would be motive enough to give. But we rather suspect that the "returns" aren't measured in dollars and cents.

Why give? It comes quite naturally, frankly, for us to receive and amass pleasures and possessions for our own delight. But Lilias challenges us with the blessedness of giving: "*first to God in surrender, then to man in sacrifice.*" She looks to the flower for example. "*The true, ideal flower is one that uses its gifts as means to an end; the brightness and sweetness are not for its own glory; they are but to attract the bees and butterflies that will fertilize and make it fruitful. All may go when the work is done—'it is more blessed to give than to receive.'*"

She expands on that principle through two other references to nature. First, she contrasts the pebble to the diamond. The one takes in all the rays of light; the other flashes them out again. Same with the opal: numerous fissures within the stone catch and refract and radiate every ray they can seize. Given to give.

We all know people who inspire us with their giving. Famous philanthropists who give back much more of their wealth than they keep for themselves. Stories are legend of people who have literally spent their lives in serving others. Just as compelling are those individuals who quietly and lovingly give of their substance, touching lives with gifts of time and service and other resources.

All such people I've ever encountered insist that they have received more than they have given. Not necessarily in tangible returns nor always in appreciation. But in the life-affirming principle that it is "more blessed to give than receive."

Less often we look at the negative. What happens when we *don't* give? What happens when we hoard and hug our treasures close to ourselves? The answer, once again, is demonstrated through the natural world. Consider the sparkling Sea of Galilee, which receives and gives out fresh water. It is alive and life giving. But follow the fresh water through the Jordan River down to the Dead Sea, which receives the water but doesn't pass it on. Without an outlet, the water stagnates. It cannot support life. It is aptly called the "dead sea."

"We ourselves are 'saved to save'—we are made to give." Lilias lived out the words she penned perhaps more radically than most of us ever will. But the choice remains the same for each of us in our own arena of living. Give or take. Sea of Galilee or the Dead Sea. Which is it to be?

Thank You, Lord, for all that You have given to me. May I not hoard these good gifts but give to others from Your generosity to me.

Living Together in Love

*With loving thoughts and words
and looks we can, as it were, twist
the threads of our lives with the
lives of others . . . that we may help
each other to be strong, like the little
strands of wool help each other,
and so we shall grow fit for God
to use us.*

—*Heavenly Light on the Daily Path*

Painting: from 1893 Journal

Two are better than one,
> because they have a good
> return for their labor:
If either of them falls down, one can help the other up . . .
> Though one may be overpowered, two can defend themselves.
A cord of three strands is not quickly broken.

—Ecclesiastes 4:9–10, 12

WHAT IS LOVE? Webster defines it as "a strong liking for or attachment or devotion to a person or persons." Books have been written to explain it, songs to exalt it, and poems to distill it. Scripture identifies different kinds of love—romantic, friendship, divine—distinguished by their respective Greek root: eros, philia, agape. Perhaps the most comprehensive definition is found in Paul's letter to the church in Corinth, where he ticks off a list of what love is or isn't, mainly in the form of action verbs.

When I checked Lilias's sources for wise words about love, I was surprised to discover that they were few and essentially unquotable, being implicitly about individuals with whom she lived and worked. Yet she lived love, and everyone took note of the fact: street urchins, young mothers who came to her for help "because she loves us," Sufi mystics who invited her into their fraternities, an Oxford don, not an adherent to the faith, who observed "I shall never forget the impression I received when I first met her; the mere look on her face and touch of her hand—made one feel that she was spiritually apart from the ordinary run of people one meets."

She did, however, offer "a lesson about living together in love" in a little booklet written for Arab women, *Heavenly Light on the Daily Path*. She observes their common activity of spinning the wool they have purchased at market. "*You take the Kerdash, pass it through patiently till every knot and tangle is cleared, and it is as soft as a cloud, and then you take the spindle and twist the threads firmly together and each little strand helps the other to hold fast till they take their place in the garment you are weaving.*"

She goes on to observe, "*Loving thoughts and words and looks . . . twist the threads of our lives with the lives of others that we may help each other to be strong, like the little strands of wool help each other and so we shall grow fit for God to use us.*"

Love is, at the end of the day, easier to observe than to describe. Perhaps one of the most memorable demonstrations of love was observed by our family several decades ago at our church missions festival. Robertson McQuilken, president of Columbia Bible College, was our keynote speaker. It became evident to all involved that his sweet-faced wife was totally dependent on him. Whenever he was out of her sight for even a moment, she would ask, "Where's Robertson? Where's Robertson?" The final evening she left her seat in the congregation "to look for Robertson" who must have momentarily been blocked from her view. He later expressed his concern adding, "This was a first."

We learned that soon afterward he had stepped down from his presidency, writing the following in a letter to his constituency:

> Recently it has become apparent that Muriel is contented most
> of the time she is with me and almost none of the time I am

away from her ... So it is clear to me that she needs me now, full-time ... The decision was made, in a way, 42 years ago when I promised to care for Muriel "in sickness and in health ... till death do us part." ... As a man of my word, integrity has something to do with it. But so does fairness. She has cared for me fully and sacrificially all these years; if I cared for her for the next 40 years I would not be out of her debt ... But there is more: I love Muriel. She is a delight to me ... I don't have to care for her. I get to!

Love is an attitude that results in action. It can sometimes lead to devoting one's entire life to a person or a cause that God has laid on our hearts. But whatever love asks of us—radical or trivial—it likewise can be manifest daily in countless ways with "*loving thoughts and works and looks*" for the people with whom we live and work. And, as the "*threads of our lives*" are twisted together in love, we all become stronger. We grow ever more fit for God's use.

What is love? We all know it when we see it. We know it when we *experience* it. Let us love others who touch our lives as we ourselves long to be loved!

Lord, twist together the threads of my life with those with whom I live and work. Shine Your love through me in "thoughts and words and looks."

Glad Light of Hospitality

It is such a happy summer with the dear bunches of the natives about the place. And there is a spirit of love all about—either I get asked out to supper at one end of the house or the other, or a plate of stew is brought to us, or a hunk of watermelon in its wonderful crimson & green—or a sugar cake or two—or my bathtowels get carried off for a private washing & come back fragrant with a scented jessamine wreath folded in—all little precious tokens—& with them the glad light of the happy spirit of help & fellowship among each other.

—Diary August 25, 1921

Painting: from Travel Journal 1893

Practice hospitality.   —Romans 12:13

IT WAS A MAGICAL EVENING. Neighbors gathered, nine-strong, on the wide back screen porch, almost other-worldly, canopied by branches of enormous live-oak trees. As we enjoyed our appetizers, the entertainment was provided by two downy owls, still babies, who flitted from branch to branch finally settling for their evening dinner just as we were called into the dining room for ours.

The table was laid in white linen, with a centerpiece of pink tulips set in a crystal vase which was flanked by candles in holders that seemed to have been cut from clear ice. I can't recall the menu (but that it was good!), yet the evening was filled with animated conversation and laughter as we explored a wide range of subjects. The candles shortened as the evening lengthened. Our hosts' next-door neighbor brought the evening to a close with these words: "This is the view that I saw nightly from the outside looking in. Now I'm on the inside looking out."

What a lovely and apt observation. For one shining evening, hospitality drew into community individuals whose primary common denominator was simply place: five cottages lining a brick-paved street. During that evening, we learned more about each other, history and hobbies, opinions and beliefs, than 365 days of quick conversations over the proverbial fence or chance encounters at the mail boxes lining our street. We departed, that evening, to go our separate ways, but also with a new sense of solidarity, of being bound together with a knowing "we'll be there for each other."

Hospitality is a golden chain linking earliest childhood to my present life, first in receiving, then in giving. I remember the excitement accompanying the words "company's coming!" and all that inferred to my child-heart. Hospitality has continued to minister to me (and mine) through all the years to follow, most profoundly at times of deepest need. Hospitality sheltered us through early years of marriage, as older couples took us under their wings, so to speak, or peers, like us, made do with the little we had then accumulated: roasting hot dogs in the fireplace of friends' unfurnished new home; sipping hot chocolate as a young mom folded laundry at her dining room table. We have been taken in for a weekend (or week!) by longtime friends and new, singles and families. We have been served by hostesses who clearly loved dressing up, pulling out fine china and silver, and creating a stunning tablescape and by others who favored the spontaneity of "come as you are to such as we are!" Little matter service or style: true hospitality embraces the guest and enriches the host!

Hospitality for Lilias was a primary means of connecting with people and embracing them in her heart. Within their first year in Algiers, Lilias and her colleagues opened the door of their small flat, in the French-speaking area of the city, for a New Year's Day tea for young Arab water-carriers with whom they made contact during their forays into town. She rejoiced when they moved into the old-city Casbah, where they could freely host local women and children in their home. During the years to follow, Lilias acquired houses along the coast and down into the Southlands, which she furnished comfortably "native-style," where people would feel at ease in familiar surrounds hosted by workers.

Dar Naama, "House of Grace," located in the nearby suburb of El Biar, initially endeared itself to Blanche and Lilias with its spacious Arab courtyard and surrounding rooms—and the dream of hosting entire Arab families during the hot summer months. After the death of Blanche, Lilias moved permanently to this home, personally realizing that dream: it became shelter for workers and Arab friends who became, in essence, her family, as indicated above in her 1921 journal entry.

Many cultures traditionally place a very high value on hospitality. The Polish have a saying, "Guest at home is equal to God at home." The ancient Greeks held that Zeus might appear in the guise of a stranger. The Chinese identified hospitality with food and food with life. Once you shared food with another, you were bound as friends. The Old Testament instructs God's people to love the stranger "for ye were strangers in the land of Egypt" (Deuteronomy 10:19 KJV). Jesus was the frequent recipient of hospitality, and the first Christians met in homes.

For too many of us, hospitality is daunting and unfortunately associated with entertainment Martha Stewart-style. But it is, in essence, love in action: opening the doors of our hearts to our guests—however they are packaged (!)—as we open the doors of our homes. It is a biblical mandate: Be "given to hospitality" (Romans 12:13 KJV). Moreover, it is a privilege and a blessing. It is a gift of ourselves—just as we are.

There are always many challenges to our time and energy. But let us pray that we may be open to how we might use our hearts and homes to embrace both friend and stranger. Just because we can't do everything doesn't mean that we can't do something.

‍➤ ➤ ➤

Thank You, God, for the countless people who have opened their hearts and lives to me. May I, in like manner, swing open the door of my heart in hospitality, embracing friend and stranger in Your love.

IN MEMORIAM: PETER CHRETIEN (NEIGHBOR)

Gladly Give

*See how this bit of oat-grass is emptying itself out. Look at the wide-openness
with which the seed-sheaths lose all that they have to yield, and then the
patient content with which they fold their hands—the content of finished
work. "She hath done what she could." Oh, the depth of rest that falls on the
soul when the voice of the Beloved speaks those words! Will they be said to us?*

—*Parables of the Cross*

I will very gladly
spend
and be spent.

Painting: from *Parables of the Cross*

I will very gladly spend and be spent for you. —2 Corinthians 12:15 KJV

IT WAS A HARVEST DINNER. People from various walks of life broke bread
together then stayed on for table fellowship. A single question was thrown out
for discussion: Name one thing for which you are thankful.

The answers were varied and, for the most part, predictable. I kept
crossing off my "choices" as people named them before my turn: family . . .

health . . . freedom . . . faith . . . The comments circled the table and came to the last in line. "I'm thankful that I am able to still be of service to others." A light shone from the eyes of a woman whom we recognized, even in our relatively short time in Mt. Dora, as a person who not only served but served with joy.

"*I will gladly spend and be spent,*" wrote Lilias on an illustration in her *Parables of the Cross*, and she proceeded to live out a lifetime of service. It is easy to look at someone like her as the exception. A called one. And yet, what is the point of life anyway if it does not include reaching out to others in love? Are we not all called to serve, in one way or another?

There are many responses to the idea of "service," from the hedonist who insists "I must take care of myself'" to those who burn out in serving others, neglecting their own basic needs. The challenge is personal and one that is in continual flux throughout the ages and stages of our lives. We (I) might aspire to the heights of Lilias's standards, but God never intended me to copy or clone another person's life of faith or service. I might be inspired, but I cannot imitate.

It has been, for me, an ongoing struggle to balance the most basic management of family, household, workplace, friendships—and on top of all that *service*. But I have, through the years, come to some understandings *about* service.

1. God never said a life of service would be easy. Realistically, to spend time and energy in the service of God is to take time and energy from other things that we might wish to be doing.

2. A need does not constitute a calling. Henri Nouwen learned this lesson the hard way. Having taught at the University of Notre Dame and the divinity schools of Yale and Harvard, written many books, and lectured extensively, he left the academic community to respond to the needs of the poor of Latin America. Through painful experience, he came to realize that though the need was compelling

and his spirit was willing, he was neither "called" nor particularly effective in that setting. His spiritual journey of soul searching is vulnerably recorded in his published diary *Road to Daybreak*. His experience illustrates a universal truth: we can't do everything.

3. Just because we can't do everything doesn't mean we can't do anything. Service is a manner of living for the Christian as it was for Christ. A habit of being. The challenge is to discern what things we are to do—to choose between good and good—and when to do them. This requires that we first seek God's direction through prayer, through listening to His voice and to our lives, and through the wisdom of godly counselors. It is often a matter of trial and error.

4. A helpful tool of discernment is to consider our "concentric circles of caring," working from the requisite relationships at the center of our lives and moving outward. During the demanding years of child rearing, for instance, family will be our greatest focus. As we tend the ongoing chores, they can become acts of service, even worship, sanctified by the spirit in which they are performed. And during those years, we can find involvement in wider circles of caring in a more limited way.

5. Rest in God's strength. Phillips Brooks said, "God does not give tasks equal to our powers, but power equal to our tasks." Translation: God does not expect us to do anything for which He will not make provision!

Grandmother Bricker took up residency with my family when she was eighty-three years old. She wanted to serve. She ironed our clothing. She assisted in meal preparation. She cleaned where and when permitted. And when she could no longer serve through working, she continued to serve through praying, for her children, her grandchildren, their friends. Her daily prayer for herself was simple: "Lord, give me life till my work is done, and give me work till my life is done."

"*I will gladly spend and be spent.*" It is a privilege to be able to serve. It is a privilege to serve. In *My Utmost for His Highest*, Oswald Chambers elaborates: "The only responsibility you have is to stay in living constant touch with God, and to see that you allow nothing to hinder your cooperation with Him . . . Wherever He places us, our one supreme goal should be to pour out our lives in wholehearted devotion to Him in that particular work . . . You are not your own. You are His."

Lord, equip me, through Your Spirit, to go beyond occasional acts of service to a manner of being, a life of serving.

Desultory Bee

A bee comforted me very much this morning concerning the desultoriness that troubles me in our work. There seems so infinitely much to be done, that nothing gets done thoroughly. If work were more concentrated, as it must be in educational or medical missions, there would be less of this— but we seem only to touch souls and leave them. And that was what the bee was doing, figuratively speaking. He was hovering among some blackberry sprays, just touching the flowers here and there in a very tentative way, yet all unconsciously, life-life-life was left behind at every touch, as the miracle-working pollen grains were transferred to the place where they could set the unseen spring working. —Diary July 9, 1907

Painting: from Diary July 9, 1907

The Spirit gives life. —John 6:63

I MUST ADMIT to resorting to Webster's dictionary upon my first reading of *desultory* in this diary entry of Lilias. This is what I found: "jumping from one thing to another; disconnected; not methodical." Could there be a better description of my varied and, yes, often random actions? It seems that my day is just that: a jumping from one activity to another, a series of disconnected endeavors, with no mind or method. It may be as simple as housekeeping activities: settle down to one task only to be diverted by the buzz of the dryer (must get those clothes out immediately) or the ring of the phone. I may sit down to attend a writing or study project only to go in search of a related resource, which pulls me off into several other related readings. And that's just the start of a day.

Reality. Often I reach the end of day and wonder: what have I done today that has any lasting significance? Well, any significance, lasting or, for that matter, immediate?! How does one measure the worth of actions that are repetitive and without apparent results? An e-mail or letter (often long overdue) finally written and mailed, a telephone conversation, a visit or meal with a friend, a meeting attended, a service performed, a deadline met, a blog post attempted?!

And then that little "desultory bee" comforts me. It really doesn't matter what I accomplish or how that activity is regarded by myself or others. What matters is that I am surcharged, like that bee, with potential life. When I draw upon the source of Life, like the bee touching the life-giving pollen in its disconnected hoverings, I receive "life" that can be transferred to whomever wherever my random actions may take me.

I do not discount the importance of the stewardship of time, of planning effective work strategies. But the best of plans are often foiled and even the finest accomplishments appear futile or ephemeral. The most important thing I can do, each and every day, is to wait upon God, to listen to Him through His Word and His world, and allow Him to surcharge me with Life. The rest is over to God.

> *We have only to see to it that we are surcharged, like the bees, with*
> *potential life. It is God and His eternity that will do the work. Yet He*
> *needs His wandering desultory bees.*   —Diary July 9, 1907

> **Lord, let me draw deeply from Your reserve of love that in my most**
> **random activities I will leave Your life-giving pollen at every touch.**

Day of Small Things

Such a day of small things still, but on God's time, & and that is enough: size as well as time & space count nothing with Him. —January 1, 1902

Painting: from Travel Journal 1900

Who has despised the day of small things? —Zechariah 40:10 NKJV

A DAY OF SMALL THINGS. It seems that many of my days are made up of just that: small things.

Take today. What has dominated the hours of this day? What have I accomplished? Answer: a disconnected trail of seemingly insignificant things. Household tasks: sorting stacks of papers; cleaning surfaces of tables, counters, and desks; feeding a cat, feeding ourselves—setting up and washing up from the same; watering plants and cutting flowers. Oh, yes, several phone conversations and e-mails and attending to small (yes, *small* again) business matters. Some reading, some writing. The list goes on: unmemorable and unmeasurable "small things" slowly lap up the hours of my day.

Lilias provides perspective to "small things" bringing them into focus: *"small things still, but on God's time, and that is enough."* The context of her words was ministry and the smallness of their efforts against the enormity of the task. Specifically, at the time of her writing, she faced a journey into the Southlands, intending to set up a small substation as a base for ministry. This mission, begun with optimism and high hopes, was fraught with setbacks and complications, ultimately forcing them to abort their plans. She was comforted by the knowledge that their best efforts were, at best, subject to "God's timing"—and that was enough.

When I first read these words, a couple of decades past, we were in the midst of pastoral ministry: living in the manse one block from the church. Lilias's words brought perspective and comfort to both of us as we considered the magnitude of our calling: he to the pastorate, me to a supportive role. There were seasons that anchored the church calendar (Advent, Lent); activities that defined the weeks and months (sermons, Bible studies, committee meetings, pastoral counseling); events that highlighted the routines (mission festivals, family retreats, annual vacation Bible school, and, of course, baptisms, weddings, and funerals). At start.

But the daily reality was that this so-called "high calling" was, in fact, sabotaged by "small things": conversations, planned and unplanned, about trivial concerns . . . tension in a relationship or fracture of a family . . . hours tending to menial chores (tending thermostats, turning off lights, and locking doors) . . . The list goes on and on. So many hours spent in doing seemingly insignificant things.

How does one measure ministry disrupted by so many seemingly insignificant tasks? How does one measure the value of one's work—any work—disrupted by seemingly unrelated distractions? (After all, is not ministry the operative context for any disciple? Is not discipleship a way of living—in God's time? Kairos.)

Whether in a life set aside for full-time ministry or a lifestyle of lay ministry, the answer is the same. We cannot measure results. My question is irrelevant. What is important is that we do anything—*everything*—required of us without calculating the results. They can't be measured. We are to be faithful to what we are assigned, big and small, and to do each thing on His terms, in His time. The results are given over to Him.

This is both liberating and challenging—at every stage in life. There is, of course, the grand vision, but the implementation of the same is made up of "small things." Like an artist cleaning the brushes and preparing the canvas for a great masterpiece. Finger exercises for the concert pianist. The early years of childhood and youth will be defined by obedience . . . student years by exams and deadlines . . . career and/or parenting years by tiny tasks, sacrifice, caring, and generosity often unobserved . . . retirement will pioneer uncharted territory with unique opportunities and challenges . . . Small things.

Small things, but in God's time. That is our daily, our constant, challenge. *"And that is enough."*

Lord, so many hours of my day are taken up with seemingly small things. May I not measure worth by size but by faithfulness to what You have assigned me to do.

Part 7

Images of Refreshment

Rest from the Press of Service

We felt that we must get our bit of quiet in the garden today, for soul as well as body—yesterday there was scarcely leisure "so much as to eat." He makes the scraps of aloneness very very precious—and though there is no possibility of having a key or of ensuring the quiet lasting for a moment, one gets a sense among the palms and fruit blossoms that one has so far as possible shut the door. And it is true as of old that "the doors being shut, came Jesus."

—Travel Journal 1895

Painting: from Travel Journal 1900

[Jesus said,] "Come with me by yourselves to a quiet place and get some rest."

—Mark 6:31

AT THE OUTBREAK of the First English Civil War (1642), Baron Astley of Reading joined with King Charles and subsequently was appointed commander of the Royalist infantry. His prayer at the Battle of Edgehill has gone down in history along with his cause: "O Lord! Thou knowest how busy I must be this day. If I forget you, do not forget me."

Too busy to pray! How many times have I faced my daily battles with that attitude if not those very words? While I would never admit to being "too busy to pray," that has been far too often my reality. Here is my varied rationale. The urgency of the moment; this matter cannot wait. (Translation: God can wait.) Or limited time: so much to do, so little time in which to do it. (Translation: My immediate concern is more important than time alone with God.) Better yet, I can pray as I work. (Translation: God is always good for "talk on the run.")

All the above is true. There are certain things that just can't wait: meal preparations, the urgent needs of a child or elderly parent, appointments to keep, deadlines to meet. And there definitely are days in which there are not enough hours to complete nonnegotiable tasks. Fact is, God *will* always be there for me. He will wait. Furthermore, what is wrong with "talking on the run"? Aren't we commanded to "pray without ceasing" (1 Thessalonians 5:17 KJV)? Some of my best praying takes place in the car, on a bike ride, in the shower.

Yes. All the above is true. But it misses the point. What is prayer? It is so much more than talking to God. It is, in fact, communion with God. Prayer keeps us in relationship with Him. And, as with any deep and growing relationship, conversation best takes place when we withdraw from our activities and spend time alone with the one with whom we wish to commune. While we can, and should, continue to converse with God throughout our waking hours, nothing can replace, in quality, time set aside on a regular basis to be alone with God. As in marriage—or one's closest friendships—for the relationship to flourish, we need more than a "tip of the hat" in passing or a quick "head's up" on our activities. We need regular time, set aside, just to be together. So with God. As E. Herman said, in *Creative Prayer*, "Prayer is the response of our whole being to the call of God. In it the soul stands at attention."

Lilias penned her need and resolve to get a "bit of quiet" in the context of extreme stress. In 1895 she and her colleague Blanche Haworth began what would be their most ambitious expedition, five months in duration. They traveled in camel caravan along the steep mountainside of the Aurès followed by a three-day journey southward, deep into the desert, to their destination, the district of the Djerid. They pitched their tent on the edge of a palm garden, in Touzer, a village just inside the border of Tunisia. For two weeks running, visitors streamed to the doorway of their tent, in groups of eight to twenty, from morning to night. They begged the women to read to them from the Scriptures and exhibited a spirit of thoughtful listening. At times, as much for the soul as for the body, Lilias was compelled to send them away so that she could get a sorely needed "bit of quiet." And, it was there, in that quiet that . . . "*came Jesus.*"

Jesus knew His disciples' need for time alone with Him. After they had been commissioned by Him to go out, "two by two," they came back to Jesus to report all that they did and taught. Even as people with pressing need gathered around them, Jesus extended to His disciples this invitation: "Come with me by yourselves to a quiet place and get some rest" (Mark 6:31). Furthermore, Jesus recognized His own need to be alone with His Father. Later that very day, after feeding the five thousand, Jesus sent His disciples off on a boat. Then "after leaving them, he went up on a mountainside [*by himself*] to pray" (Mark 6:46).

I have to ask myself: if Jesus, who was at once human and divine, felt it necessary to draw apart from the crowds and His closest friends to spend time alone with God—to recharge, to find the nourishment and strength to carry out His partnership with God on earth—who do I think I am to believe I can survive without fellowship with God the Father?

I *need* time alone with God—"a bit of quiet"—to renew my spirit, to regain perspective, to restore my relationship with Him. I must seek solitude. Like everything else of importance, if I don't schedule it into my life, it will be scheduled out by default. There will be times that my best intentions will be sabotaged by factors beyond my control. But I must never forget that in those priceless "*scraps of aloneness*" comes Jesus. *He* is essential for my soul's survival.

"Be still, and know that I am God" (Psalm 46:10).

God, I seek a bit of quiet to be alone with You amid the busyness of this day.
I'm grateful that even if I fail to remember You, You never forget me.

Rest for the Soul

Oh, the desert is lovely in its restfulness. The great brooding stillness over and through everything is so full of God. One does not wonder that He used to take His people out into the wilderness to teach them. —Diary March 6, 1895

Painting: from Travel Journal 1895

Come to me, all you who are weary and burdened, and I will give you rest. Take my yoke upon you and learn from me, for I am gentle and humble in heart, and you will find rest for your souls.

—Matthew 11:28–29

LILIAS LOVED THE DESERT. She loved its people who lived out their lives in the most basic battle for sustenance and survival. She loved the desert's brooding beauty with its long stretches of open spaces and its clear star-filled skies. She loved its *"lovely . . . restfulness."* Little wonder, given her usual crowded and cluttered conditions of everyday living in the Casbah, that she found the great stillness of the desert *"so full of God."* So intense, for her, was the lure of the desert that she tested her desire to return to the Southlands to see that it was of God.

She was not alone, nor the first, in her craving for the desert. Egyptian hermits of the fourth and fifth centuries—desert fathers—withdrew themselves from the activity of society to seek the calm and rest of the desert. Here, apart from the commerce and business of everyday living, they could reclaim their true selves and encounter the love of God. So rich was the learning of their solitude that people made pilgrimage to seek their desert wisdom. "Seek God," said Abba Sisoes, "and not where God lives."

For the thirty-seven years of Sundays that I worshiped in my Lake Wales church, I was handed a weekly bulletin that featured these words on the cover: "To all who are weary and need rest; to all who are lonely and want fellowship; to all who mourn and need comfort; to all who pray and to all who do not, but ought; to all who sin and need a Savior; and to whosoever will come—this church opens wide the door and says in the name of the Lord Jesus, 'Welcome.'" And always, almost without fail, each time I read those rest-promising words, I would experience a little catch in my heart. For this was, of course, a liberal paraphrase of Jesus's gentle words, "Come to me, all you who are weary and burdened, and I will give you rest . . . *rest for your souls*" (Matthew 11:28–29, emphasis added).

Rest for the soul. Each of us, most likely, has a place in our mind that represents the "desert rest" that Lilias craved. And yet, in reality, rare are those places of rest, and few and far between in our everyday existence. Even when we actually experience our brand of "desert rest," well, we take ourselves with us—our restless and fractured and fragmented selves.

Is there ever a time when we are free from the clutter and noise of busy lives and restless hearts? The student years with deadlines and demands . . . the early years of career-building forging one's way while burning the midnight oil . . . the family years and all the related actions and activities requisite to raising our young to leave us . . . the empty nest, then retirement with the increased care of parents, to say nothing of the sheer maintenance of our own bodies and homes.

With or without the desert—real or figurative—the rest for which we all long must transcend our circumstances, or we will forever be tossed to and fro by whatever winds assail us. We must create our own deserts—our own sanctuaries of the soul—within which we can create the emotional and spiritual space that allows for the presence of God.

The Russian mystic Theophane the Recluse said, "To pray is to descend with the mind into the heart, and there to stand before the face of the Lord, ever-present, all seeing, within you." It is God, and God alone, who can give us true rest, rest for our souls.

Let us draw a circle of quiet around our hearts and welcome God into that space. Let us "descend with the mind into the heart, and . . . stand before the face of the Lord." Let us catch up with our souls as He brings true rest to our hearts.

➤ ➤ ➤

Quiet my restless heart, O Lord. Come into my being and fill me with Your Spirit. Give me rest for my soul.

Facing Our Miseries with God

"With God"—these are the wonderful words, this is the wonderful fact that changes earth's sordid surroundings into the heavenly places where we are seated with Him.

—The Letter "M"

Painting: from Pocket Sketchbook, Algeria, 1888

I have learned the secret of being content in any and every situation, whether . . . living in plenty or in want. I can do everything through him who gives me strength.

. . . And my God will meet all your needs according to his glorious riches in Christ Jesus.   —Philippians 4:12–13, 19

I APPROACHED MY friend's home with fear and trembling. It was my turn to provide the evening meal after her return home from rehab. She had recovered fully from a previous stroke—been reinstated at work—only to suffer an even more debilitating combination of stroke and heart attack. She was back home only to start all over again.

I was welcomed with a warm smile, urged to sit down—"the food can wait"—and we spent a joy-filled hour catching up with the activities of our adult children and the various events of our lives. Before leaving I had to ask: "I'd been told that you would minister to me. Tell me, what is the secret of your contentment?"

Her answer was not glib. She told of her despair upon her first stroke: worry over income (how would she pay the bills?); fears for the future (would she recover? would she get her job back?). She entertained self-pitying thoughts (why me? why this?). Reluctantly she began the long road of rehabilitation: daily physical therapy, regular counseling sessions. The first week in group therapy, the counselor put the facts bluntly: life had dealt them a severe blow, the road to recovery was long and painful. The prognosis uncertain. He drew a large rectangle on a white board. "This was before." Then he drew a smaller rectangle within the larger. "Your world has become more limited. You may never be able to do some of the things you did before. It may be harder to do other things. But you have a choice. Regardless of the size of the perimeter of your box, you can choose to live fully, to the very edge of those limits. And, in that choice, you are like every other person."

Barb made a sweeping gesture indicating the boundaries of her small living room. "I have everything I need. Shelter, food, friends." She pointed to framed pictures on shelves, "Family—children, grandchildren." Then she crossed her hands over her heart, "And, I have God. With Him I am never alone."

I left her that day, blessed and challenged. I reflected on areas of discontent in my life, so insignificant compared to what my friend was experiencing. I asked myself, what are the contentment chasers in my life? What are the disturbers of the peace, *my* peace? Usually it is the result of factors so subtle that I'm unaware, at the time, of their effect on my inner well-being. Expectations: foiled or dashed. Comparisons: not having as much or doing as well as someone else. Disappointments: things didn't turn out as I hoped or expected. Setbacks: sometimes entirely out of my control, sometimes of my own making. The list could go on and on, I suppose, fueled by the unpredictable circumstances of a given day.

I look at the richness within the perimeters of my life. My given. I consider all the possibilities of life and work and love therein. I know that it is, by the grace of God, what it is today; and I know that there are no guarantees that it will remain the same. (Truth is, the longer one lives, the more certain the possibility of limitations.) But regardless of the size of the box I call my life, one thing is certain: it is and can always be "with God."

During Lilias's years in North Africa, as a growing number of workers united in her vision, she developed an in-house magazine titled *El Couffa*—Arabic for "an open basket"—in which were gathered bits of information and inspiration, news local and international to circulate among the stations and outposts. It featured an editorial column, "The Letter 'M'," with pithy advice to missionaries. In Letter V, "Missionaries and Their Miseries," she asked the question: "*What are our miseries? Shall we make a list of them and what shall we write opposite to them? Shall it be 'this is very hard' or shall it be 'with God'?*"

She concludes with this story. "*A friend told of me that she knew an old charwoman who lived in a little garret in great poverty. One day speaking of returning to her room after a day's work, she said, 'And as I open the door I find the dear Lord waiting there for me, and I say to myself, "can Heaven be better!"'*"

What are my miseries? What shall I write opposite them? Shall it be "*this is very hard*" or shall it be "*with God*"?

Lord, You know the challenges and difficulties I face today.
I know that nothing is too hard to handle "with God."

The Purity God Wants

I had a time with Aissha alone. Her soul was clouded and I could get no response heavenward. She was preparing to go, winding her coarse white

Painting: from Diary 1906

haik round her. I could only call silently on God for some touch. Then her eyes rested on a vase of flowers on the table—celandines from the lanes, and cream and gold jonquils from the fields. I said, "How pure they are— that is the purity that God wants." She looked up with her face soft and shining, "Yes, I should like the life of Jesus in me to be like that."

—Diary February 21, 1906

Create in me a pure heart, O God,
    and renew a steadfast spirit within me.   —Psalm 51:10

A LIFETIME AGO, or so it seems, Sunday morning was the most difficult time of my week. I was left alone to prepare three little children for church, their father being safely ensconced in his study at church, putting final touches on his sermon. This morning, in particular, it seemed almost a travesty to offer thanks for the food, the children being "at" each other from the very moment they awakened. In a last-ditch attempt to redeem the morning, I suggested we "ask Jesus to forgive us and give us a brand-new start." With a collective sense of relief, they agreed, and one could almost feel the air clear with the final "Amen."

Later that day, I rushed about trying to put the house in order for a meeting. Time was short and so was my temper. The children were "too much with me." But single-mindedly I kept to task, pressing forward toward my goal. Young David, who had been around the edges of things, stilled me with a question: "Mommy? Do you want to stop right now and ask Jesus for a brand-new start?"

There was no mistaking the implications of his suggestion nor the earnestness with which he offered a solution. I checked the impulse to come to my own defense: too much to do; too little time in which to do it. Humbled, I apologized, and together we took a moment to ask Jesus "for a new start for Mommy."

Who doesn't love a brand-new start?! Often this is an opportunity associated with fresh beginnings on our calendars: a new day, new season, new year. Sometimes it is a new job or house or locale. Whether it is the blank slate of a calendar or the changes that accompany a new place or space, we anticipate "a brand new start" with all its fresh prospects and possibilities.

There is a yet deeper, more profound new start than that associated with the blank pages of a calendar or the challenge of new opportunities. It is the new start of a brand-new heart.

Such was the challenge facing Lilias as she came alongside the Arab girls who peopled her life. Girlhood was brought to an abrupt end with early marriages. The brides, in turn, were often cast aside for yet younger women when scarcely out of their teens, leaving them vulnerable and subject to unthinkable difficulties, physical, emotional, and spiritual.

So it was with Aissha from the nearby village of Blida. Young, pretty and separated from her husband for two months, she was living alone and had become visibly *"flighty"*—if not worse—definitely exhibiting a show of pride and temper. Sensing that she was distancing spiritually, Lilias longed to penetrate her *"cloudy soul,"* praying silently for *"some touch"* from God.

The opportunity presented itself at the end of a seemingly unproductive visit. Just as Aissha was leaving, her eyes rested on a vase of flowers—*"celandines from the lanes, and cream and gold jonquils from the fields."* Lilias observed, *"How pure they are—that is the purity that God wants."*

Aissha's response was immediate: "*She looked up with her face soft and shining. 'Yes, I should like the life of Jesus in me to be like that.'*"

Lilias answered, "*Yes, they came pure and sweet out of the black muddy earth, without a soil on them. Shall we pray that you may be like them?*" Together they prayed, Aissha's head resting on Lilias's shoulder, asking for the forgiveness that results in a brand-new start, pure and sweet like the flowers gathered from lane and field.

At times we long for a brand-new start, "*pure and sweet,*" in the deepest places of the soul. Such a start is the promise of Scripture, but it comes with a caveat. *Repentance.* Not only for the "big sins" but more often for the subtle attitudes and actions that inoculate our consciences and cloud our souls: indifference to God, irritability and impatience with the people with whom we live and work, pride, harboring a grudge, dissatisfaction with our "lot" in life, jealousy or envy for those who seem to fare better than ourselves. We want refreshment of Spirit but often resist the very conditions requisite for the same. Yet when we humble our spirits and acknowledge both the sin that clouds our relationship with God and our helplessness to correct the situation on our own, we are ready to receive His wonderful gift of forgiveness. "Repent, then, and turn to God, so that your sins may be wiped out, that times of refreshing may come from the Lord" (Acts 3:19).

A new year. A brand-new start. Yes, but may it be deeper than mere experience: plans, goals, resolutions. May it begin in a pure heart that meets the requisite conditions—contrition followed by repentance—thus receiving the refreshment that comes from the Lord.

Create in me a clean heart, O God; and renew a right spirit within me.
Cast me not away from thy presence; and take not thy holy spirit from me.
Restore unto me the joy of thy salvation; and uphold me with thy free spirit.
Amen.   —Psalm 51:10–12 KJV

A Sad That Won't Go Away

The beauty of that line of Hebrew poetry came afresh today. The thickest of the cloud storm would be just where He is passing. We see the dust now. We shall see His Footprints when He has passed along the way.

—Diary August 17, 1919, and September 20, 1924

Painting: from Journal 1896–1897

And my God will meet all your needs according to his glorious riches in Christ Jesus. —Philippians 4:19

HOW DOES ONE PREPARE oneself or someone else for the inevitable blows of life? Many years ago a tragedy struck our small southern town, claiming the lives of four children in one family. Our community was devastated by this mother's loss, as was our family. Our lives had been interwoven with theirs. We were without words or consolation.

The schools brought in counselors to help classmates process this loss. And we, as parents, tried to determine what effect it had particularly on our oldest son who had been in a children's club with one of the girls.

One day I noticed him on the front porch sitting quietly on a rocking chair, an uncharacteristic posture for this active boy. I joined him and pressed the question: "How are you doing?"

"Okay, I guess." Then he added, "I just have a sad inside that won't go away."

A sad that won't go away. One cannot turn on the television, radio, or computer these days without witnessing the unbearable sufferings of families who mourn loved ones. No satisfactory answers have been given or resolutions provided that ease the reality of massive loss. One cannot go through life in avoidance of the reality of staggering suffering, for ourselves or for others.

What do we do with a "sad that won't go away"?

This question was addressed, in part, for me by an unexpected source. I was driving to the grocery store listening to a speaker who captivated my attention from the start as he talked about sadness. His compelling words enticed me to sit in my car and listen to him talk to the end, wanting to know who he was. He talked about "sadness" as an appropriate response to loss. He differentiated between clinical depression (for which professional help even, at times, medication was appropriate) and the everyday brand of depression that is, in fact, an appropriate feeling of sadness in response to loss. The degree of "sadness" (depression) is usually in proportion to the loss, but the loss itself can be small or immense. Loss is loss.

He illustrated how even a relatively "small" loss can result in a surprisingly significant sense of depression. With the unaccustomed royalty for a book he authored, he bought for the first time ever a new car off a sales lot with all the bells and whistles, to say nothing of color choice, exterior and interior. On his way to a speaking engagement, he stopped at a pharmacy to pick up a prescription. Driving over the curb, he hit an unbending concrete trash container. He heard the crush of metal. The fender was bent. What had begun as a merry drive to a happy destination continued as a dark journey with a heavy heart.

His name was Dr. Archibald Hart, and he was talking about themes of his book *Unlocking the Mystery of Your Emotions*. After telling this story to a live audience, he had asked his audience, "What do you think was the loss that triggered my depression?" The answers had been varied. Loss of pride, of money, of time . . . Then one person suggested, "Loss of perfection. It will never be perfect again." Hart recalled that tears had inexplicably welled up in his eyes as this young man inadvertently hit on a nerve that even he, the distinguished psychologist, had not considered. The man was right. His car for one shining, short moment had been perfect. And it never would be again.

His point was this: if something so very trivial could "make him sad," one might imagine the emotional power of something more significant. He wanted his audience to understand and embrace a sadness for what it is: an appropriate response to an event or situation.

Where did we ever get the idea that we are always to be happy? We live in a culture that specializes in a host of gimmicks to distract, avoid, sublimate, medicate, or eliminate all manner of discomfort. And yet, way down deep in our souls, we know that we can't truly pass through this world and escape pain or suffering or, at the least, discomfort. Nor can we avoid the fear of the same.

Scripture speaks of a joy that transcends circumstances, but it does not promise immunity from difficulty. It is only as we accept our true feelings, of fear or sadness or depression, that we can even begin to deal with those emotions.

There is no escape from "a sadness inside that does not go away," but there is a promise of Someone who will walk through that sadness with us, Someone who will not leave us comfortless, who has walked this earth before us and experienced every emotion common to humankind.

During a time of great difficulty, Lilias saw with spiritual vision a perspective, taken from a line of Hebrew poetry, that illuminated her darkness and speaks to us today: "*The thickest of the cloud storm would be just where He is passing,*" adding, "*We see the dust now. We shall see His Footprints when He has passed along the way.*"

Lord, I know that there is no exemption from suffering in this broken world. Please come alongside me in Spirit and be my sufficiency.

Sing!

*I have been finding a great
blessedness in these last few
months in definitely obeying
the command "Let them sing
aloud upon their beds!"—I
remembered Pearsall Smith
half a lifetime ago, saying in a
meeting—at the first Oxford
Conference or thereabout—
that he wondered how many
present had ever obeyed it. But
the seed thought has never got
vitalized til now.*

—Diary February 5, 1919

I will sing and make music.

—Psalm 57:7

Painting: from Journal 1898

AMY CARMICHAEL, in *Whispers of His Power*, posits the question: "Do you ever find prayer difficult because of tiredness or dryness?" She suggests, "When that is so, it is an immense help to let the psalms and hymns we know by heart say themselves or sing themselves inside us. This is possible anywhere and at any time." Lilias took this a step further, quoting the biblical injunction "Let them sing aloud upon their beds" (see Psalm 149:5), making it a daily practice upon awakening in the morning.

It is interesting to note that this began decades after it was first suggested to Lilias at an Oxford Convention. The context is all important in understanding why, after all these years, Lilias turned to a previously unheeded practice. The year was 1918. Lilias and her colleague Blanche Haworth made a return trip to Tozeur, after a twenty-two-year absence. Thrilled to see the same spirit of receptivity, they rented a fondak (ancient inn) and prepared it for a desert out-station. Then, stepping out in faith, they identified yet another post in Monastir, along the coastline of Tunisia, to sustain workers during the hottest months of the summer. Energized by this new development, they returned to Algiers and resumed their somewhat curtailed wartime programs, writing, and hospitality, all the while strategizing future ministry in the Southlands.

Then, without warning, Blanche had developed a fever, not considered serious, that escalated into a fatal illness. On March 9, 1918, the morning of the thirtieth anniversary of their arrival in Algeria, Blanche *"crossed to the other side all unknowing."* Not only had Lilias lost her beloved friend, united in vision and service from the first day in Algeria, but a colleague indispensable to the ongoing ministry. Visions for the future were curtailed as Lilias reorganized the forces to accommodate the pressing needs at home. Lilias moved from the Casbah in Algiers to the suburb of El Biar to sustain Blanche's ministry of hospitality to local families and the constant stream of guests.

Lilias's coworkers marveled at her strength and grace as she threw herself into the various ministries and dealt with the reality of "hope deferred" in future plans. But the unpublished pages of her diaries took on a more personal turn as she explored the mysteries of heaven. What did it look like? (Would Blanche be welcomed by the *"dear baby souls"* taken in a typhoid epidemic?) She pondered the theories of paradise (waking or sleeping?) and considered the ever-diminishing barrier between earth and eternity. Almost lost, among her musings and reports of ministry, is this cryptic paragraph that reveals the dullness of her aching soul: *"One's first waking then has been heretofore so constantly a time of fighting through to a place where one could pray but . . . praising & praising the Precious Blood & the name of Jesus every drift of mist melts away & prayer can begin straight away under a clear sky."*

There are times when we don't feel like praying. The loss of a loved one or a way of life has sealed our hearts. Our lips are mute. Difficulties that we face daily have worn down our spirits or made doubters of us. Why pray? Sometimes there are stretches of dullness, even depression, that make the effort of praying seemingly impossible. Even if we want to pray, we can't. Can something as simple as a song turn our thoughts to praise and our praise to prayer?

Amy Carmichael maintained, "Hymns, little prayer-songs of our own, even the simplest of them, can sing us into His love. Or more truly, into the consciousness of His love for we are never for one moment out of it."

A friend who was undergoing chemo treatment shared her particular dread of the MRIs, her claustrophobic fear of the tunnel. Her antidote? The deeper into the clanging tunnel, the louder she sang a chorus from childhood. Her prayer-tunes out-sang the fears and sounds of the machine.

Many of us, like my friend, have a memory "deposit" of hymns—which serve as "valuable reserves hidden away for us to draw on," to use the metaphor found in *Spiritual Moments with the Great Hymns*. Sometimes the prompter of a hymnbook can help us express the words our mouths can't seem to form. From time to time, I have turned to *The One Year Book of Hymns* as a personal devotional, reading the daily story behind the hymn then (quietly!) intoning the words of praise that lead me to prayer.

Can it really be so simple—a song, a prayer? Certainly we grasp the importance of corporate singing—campfire, church, cathedral—from the earliest of time. Psalms, considered the first prayerbook, were set to music and sung by pilgrims of old. But solo? Me alone with God? Can singing lift the dullness from my soul and turn my words to prayer? Richard Foster writes: "The medium of music gives wings to our words and freedom to our devotion."

Can singing turn one's heart from dullness to praise? From praise to prayer? Try it! Sing when you don't feel like praying. Sing till you do feel like praying. Sing your praise. Sing out of the gloom. Sing for obedience. Sing for the glory of God. Sing! "I will sing to the Lord . . . The Lord is my strength and my song" (Exodus 15:1–2).

I sing praise to You, O God. Take the dullness from my soul and turn my words to grateful praise.

A Listening Heart

*I have found a corner in Fortification Woods, only five minutes from the
house, where every one is quite out of sight, and I go there every morning with
my Bible . . . it is so delicious on these hot spring mornings and God rests one
through it for the whole day, and speaks so through all living things.*

—Journal Letters

Painting: Undated

Be still, and know that I am God.   —Psalm 46:10

FRANCIS BACON WROTE, "God has two textbooks—Scripture and
Creation—and we would do well to listen to both." Lilias "read" God's Work
alongside His Word. She saw lessons in its design and processes that revealed
to her the Creator, nourishing her beauty-loving spirit as well as her God-
loving soul. Her diaries and journals are filled with lessons from the natural
world illuminated with her watercolors:

The daisies have been talking again . . .
The word of the Lord came on a dandelion . . .
The martins have been reading me a faith lesson . . .
The snow is speaking . . .
I was much comforted this morning by a shaft of sunlight
that came with sunrise.

The created always whispers and sometimes shouts its Maker pointing us continually from the seen to the unseen, if only we attend. And I ask myself: Am I listening? Do I allow God's voice to speak through the natural world as well as through His revealed Word? What does it take for me to hear?

While there is no simple prescription, I suspect it begins with an attentive eye and a listening heart. In poetry Elizabeth Barrett Browning captured this reality:

> Earth's crammed with heaven,
> And every common bush afire with God;
>> But only he who sees, takes off his shoes,
>> The rest sit round it and pluck blackberries.

The challenge is implicit: Stop. Look. Listen!

God, give me a listening heart. Speak through Your Word and Your world.

Part 8

Images of Faith

You Must Keep Moving Forward

The word God has given is "passing through." Passing "through" the broken-up gate (Micah) Passing "through" the stoning crowd (Luke). Passing "through" the wall of waves (Hebrews 11). "By faith, they passed through"—not on one side, avoiding the place of difficulty, but through.

—Diary November 13, 1902

Painting: from Diary 1906

When you pass through the waters,
    I will be with you;
And when you pass through the rivers,
    they will not sweep over you.   —Isaiah 43:2

PASSING THROUGH DIFFICULTY. Not around, avoiding the source of pain, but through it. There really are no short cuts through difficulty. I think back to the example of my parents, decades ago, when I was in college. Acute financial reverses left them few choices. Bankruptcy or the long, seemingly impossible task of paying back each creditor, with no immediate source of income. I watched as they sent out the carefully (prayerfully) crafted letter promising each person/corporation that they would pay their creditors equally, as the money came in, until their debts were resolved. I don't know over how many years that process took place, but I do recall when we, with my parents, offered a prayer of thanksgiving, the last payment paid. Passing through . . .

I remember a particularly difficult time in ministry when it became obvious that all the explanations and efforts on our part (and of the staff) were not sufficient to satisfy our critics. Every "solution" had a problem, and it seemed that there was not a plausible way out of the situation. But to simply keep on keeping on . . . regardless of discouragement, in spite of misunderstanding . . . During that time, I consulted my mother, who gave words of counsel that were backed by life experience: "You just keep moving forward with what you need to do, for your family, for the church, for yourself, and leave the rest in God's hands." Passing through . . .

These two situations, reported in brief, are insignificant compared to the suffering I have witnessed through forty-five years of ministry. But the reality is the same: there is no shortcut through suffering. The loss of a loved one, betrayal of a spouse or friend, disease, the disgrace of a family member . . .

Suffering for (and from) others—with (or without) fault of one's own— comes in different shapes and sizes. But the reality is the same: there is no shortcut through suffering. *"By faith, they passed* through'—*not on one side, avoiding the place of difficulty, but* through."

Lilias draws on Old and New Testament texts to underscore that reality. She refers to deliverance promised the remnant of Israel when their King (Messiah) would break down the gates and go out before them to Jerusalem (Micah); Jesus's walking through the crowds of angry people (Luke); the children of Israel passing through the wall of waves of the Red Sea on dry ground (Hebrews).

Suffering is a given of our broken world. "We say that there ought to be no sorrow, but there is sorrow, and we have to accept and receive ourselves in its fires," wrote Oswald Chambers in *My Utmost for His Highest* (June 25). "If we try to evade sorrow, refusing to deal with it, we are foolish. Sorrow is one of the biggest facts in life, and there is no use in saying it should not be."

The "why?" of suffering is beyond the purpose of this reflection and, for that matter, my intellectual grasp. (See Philip Yancey's *Disappointment with God*; C. S. Lewis's *The Problem of Pain*.) But Scripture repeatedly addresses the "how" of experiencing difficulty. There are many reassurances for the believer on the path through suffering. Jesus, Himself, embraced fully our pain through His life on earth and His death on the cross. Moreover, He promised "I will never leave you." He will be there for us, in the midst of our pain, if we reach out to Him.

Face it: no one really wants to suffer. But in the midst of the inevitability of the same, we do have a choice: to learn what we can from it—about ourselves, about God, about others—or waste it. As C. S. Lewis noted in *The Problem of Pain*, "If the world is indeed a 'vale of soul-making,' it seems on the whole to be doing its work."

God, although there is no shortcut through suffering, I know You will be present with us. Strengthen me to embrace the pain and learn from it the lessons You wish to teach me.

Deep Waters

"I am come into deep waters" took on a new meaning this morning. It started with perplexing matters concerning the future. Then it dawned that shallow waters were a place where you can neither sink nor swim, but in deep waters it is one or the other: "waters to swim in"—not to float in. Swimming is the intense, most strenuous form of motion—all of you is involved in it—and every inch of you is in abandonment of rest upon the water that bears you up. —December 20, 1927

Painting: Undated

Help us, O LORD our God; for we rest on thee, and in thy name we go.
—2 Chronicles 14:11 KJV

DEEP WATERS. A place physically where one can neither touch ground with feet nor grasp support with hands. The only way to keep afloat is by the exercise of strength and the abandonment of body to the water that bears it.

And so it is, spiritually speaking. Deep waters. The place interiorly where we are submerged. No place to rest. No anchor to grip. Every last effort must be given to survive. To stay afloat.

The "deep waters" to which Lilias refers concerned the future of the Algiers Mission Band. The situation unfolds in the pages of her diary. It concerned the mission of the band: were the stations (outposts along the coast and south into the interior) a means to an end (a base from which they would continue to itinerate to unreached territories) or ends in themselves (developing and maintaining existing programs)? At the heart of the concern, Lilias believed, were issues of faith: the physical risk of penetrating deeper into territories beyond the reach of outposts and the financial risk of funding their new ventures.

The stakes were high. Clearly she believed that their mission was to *"launch out into the deep, out of reach of any landing place, if the way should prove stormy."* But the decision required unanimity of the workers, without the promise of her continuing leadership. She was already living on borrowed time, her heart out-beating the prognosis of medical experts. Furthermore, lack of consensus on this critical issue could result in a breakdown not only of mission but unity of the band. Deep waters.

Deep waters. Yes. But that is not all of the story. In deep waters it is all or nothing: sink or swim. *"Swimming is the intense, most strenuous form of motion— all of you is involved in it—and every inch of you is in abandonment of rest upon the water that bears you up."*

What was the "water" of which she wrote, the water that *"bears you up"*? Answer: "We rest on thee, and in thy name we go." The exercise of faith— *"most strenuous form of motion"*—is in the strong name of God. Deep waters— abandonment to *God*.

We, like Lilias, have our own "deep waters." It might, like her, involve some unknown future, some unforeseen development. We might find ourselves thrashing in uncharted waters, seemingly without support or solution. It might be more immediate: financial, marital, medical, vocational, relational, emotional . . . We have exhausted our resources; our energy is depleted.

This is the moment for abandonment. The moment to let go and rest *"upon the water that bears you up."* "The moment we recognize our complete weakness and our dependence upon Him will be the very moment that the Spirit of God will exhibit His power," notes Oswald Chambers in *My Utmost for His Highest* (May 5).

My husband recalls a childhood memory at the YMCA pool in Hong Kong. A string of ropes with rings were extended the entire length of the swimming pool. He would reach out for the first ring then swing to the next, working his way, ring by ring, toward the opposite end of the pool. The rush was heady; his swimming skills were insufficient should he lose his grip and fall to the depths below. But he was unafraid. His father was swimming the length of the pool, following beneath him, ready to rescue him should he fall.

Deep waters. Whether suspended precariously above deep waters or submerged within: little matter. Our heavenly Father bears us up as certainly as the earthly father who waited and watched below. Rarely do we chose "abandonment." It goes against our nature. Most often it occurs when we see no other options. All props are knocked out from under or around us. One wonders what would happen if this spirit of "abandonment" to God became our MO?!

What is the water that bears me up? "We rest on thee, and in thy name we go."

> The eternal God is your refuge,
> and underneath are the everlasting arms.
>
> —Deuteronomy 33:27

God, there are many uncertainties in my life: where to go, what to do. I release myself into Your everlasting arms, knowing that You are my strength and support.

Lesson of the Buttercup

Look at this buttercup as it begins to learn its new lesson. The little hands of the calyx clasp tightly in the bud round the beautiful petals, in the young flower their grasp grows more elastic—loosening somewhat in the daytime, but keeping the power of contracting, able to close in again during a rainstorm, or when night comes on. But see the central flower which has reached its maturity. The calyx hands have unclasped utterly now—they have folded themselves back, past all power of closing again upon the petals leaving the golden crown free to float away when God's time comes. Have we learned the buttercup's lesson yet? Are our hands off the very blossom of our life? Are all things—even the treasures that He has sanctified—held loosely, ready to be parted with, without a struggle, when He asks for them? —Parables of the Cross

Watercolor: Color plate from *Parables of the Cross*

Of thine own have we given thee. —1 Chronicles 29:14 KJV

LILIAS CALLS ATTENTION to three stages of the buttercup's life: the bud with petals tightly clasped in the calyx; the open flower retaining the power of contracting its petals; an open flower, petals folded back, golden crown, beyond the power of closing. Then, noting the flower wide open; fully exposed, she raises the question: "*Have we learned the buttercup's lesson?*" The lesson, she goes on to state, is one of total abandonment to God, like the open flower, ready to release all things when asked to do so: "*Are all things—even the treasures that He has sanctified—held loosely, ready to be parted with, without a struggle, when He asks for them?*"

Abandonment to self. Full surrender. These phrases capture a concept that runs counter to our culture's most cherished beliefs: autonomy, independence, self-determination, personal identity. These concepts run deep in our human nature. *Me* and *mine* are among the earliest words of a toddler's vocabulary.

But what if abandonment—letting go—is release to something, *Someone* better able? If I truly believed that to be the case, would it make any difference?

Throughout the many years I researched the life and works of Lilias Trotter, I was dogged by a question: Was it worth it? Did she really need to give up—let go—of a career in art that potentially could have ranked her among the great artists of her day? Isn't it possible that she could have reached even more people for Jesus through her great gift (and potential fame) than she did in the relative obscurity of North Africa, around people who did not recognize her immense talent, for whom her art had little or no currency?

I was forced to answer that very question in the home of her grand-nephew, who's taken the role of family historian. Gracious hosts, Robin and Claire hospitably shared their home and showed us various Trotter artifacts. At the end of our visit, Claire looked me in the eyes and echoed my question: "Why? Was it worth it, really? She gave so much for so little return."

Drawing from all that I knew about Lilias—her life, her call—I admitted, at first, to appreciating Claire's question. Then I noted the high regard we give to people in other professions—artist, athlete, musician, by way of example—who sacrifice everything to develop their discipline. We recognize—*admire*—their singleness of purpose. We call it "passion." Yet when the same devotion is given to the world of the spirit—*faith*—we call it "fanaticism." Lilias was fueled by her love for a particular people: their lot on earth; their destination eternally. If we believed the stakes to be eternal, as did Lilias, could we not acknowledge the nobility of her mission?

I know that Lilias's "lesson of the buttercup" was born of personal experience, a lesson fully embraced. Even as she beautifully illustrated the process by which one attains to this level of detachment, I recognized how she had come to that level of total abandonment where it was no longer sacrifice, but joy, to be set free to follow her Master's purposes, whatever, wherever that might be. Many of us remain in that middle state, opening our petals for a while, but retaining our power to contract them.

Lilias's lesson here is a gentle one. It is a gradual movement from tight control to conditional release to full abandonment. It is, at core, a lesson of trust. It is the belief that our Creator, the One who gave us all that is good in our lives, knows better how to use those "gifts" for His higher purposes and for our highest good. It is less a matter of what we give up and more a matter of to whom we release it.

In *Mere Christianity*, C. S. Lewis puts it this way:

> The principle runs through all life from top to bottom. Give up yourself, and you will find your real self. Lose your life and you will save it. Submit to death, death of your ambitions and favourite wishes every day and death of your whole body in the end: submit with every fibre of your being, and you will find eternal life. Keep back nothing. Nothing that you have not given away will be really yours. Nothing in you that has not died will ever be raised from the dead. Look for yourself, and you will find in the long run only hatred, loneliness, despair, rage, ruin, and decay. But look for Christ and you will find Him, and with Him everything else thrown in.

Decades after drawing this buttercup, Lilias looked back and rejoiced at the wonderful life God had given her. I don't know fully what the "lesson of the buttercup" means for me in the large. It certainly has not required, to date, anything close to radical, as with Lilias. But I do have a fairly good idea what it means for me today: to entrust my life, and all the people, places, plans, things that define it, fully into God's loving and trustworthy care.

> He is no fool who gives what he can't keep
> to gain what he cannot lose. —Jim Elliot

» » »

God, I entrust to You, today, my life and all the people, places, plans and things that define it. I write my signature on the blank check of my life for You to write Your will.

Are You There, God?

Do we not see sometimes that God begins, as it were, by taking the initiative and letting us simply follow on with Him. Then the obvious leading ceases. He is there, but He has withdrawn the pillar of cloud from before us, and asks us to go on in bare faith, while He is shielding and separating us in ways out of our ken, from the dangers that are seen by Him alone. —Diary January 22, 1928

Painting: from Travel Journal 1893

The LORD replied, "My Presence will go with you,
and I will give you rest." —Exodus 33:14

IT HAPPENED BEFORE and will, no doubt, happen again. My telephone conversation with son David was interrupted when, while driving, he reached a "dead zone" for his cell phone service. "Are you there, David? Are you there?" I speak into empty space.

Five minutes later, he calls me back and says, "I wonder how long I talked before realizing you weren't even there! I will have to finish later, I'm at my destination."

"That's okay," I reassure him. "I think we've been over this before. I probably already know what you were saying."

"That's good," he responds. "I don't really need to talk anymore. It was helpful just to put it into words, even if you didn't hear it!"

We had a good laugh over our "disconnect." Then we hung up and carried on with our separate lives. But it is not quite so funny when the perceived "disconnect" is with God.

"Are you there, God?" is often the question of our hearts. "Can You hear me? Are You really listening? Do You even care?" Sometimes it seems as if our prayers go out into the cyberspace, to no avail. Is anyone on the listening end?

Probably most of us, if we are truly honest, experience times, even seasons of times, when we do not sense the presence of God. Pray as we may, with all our hearts, and He doesn't seem to respond. Sometimes it is when we feel we need Him most, for direction, for comfort, for help. And our hearts cry, "Are You there, God?"

It is to that very condition—the seeming absence of God—that Lilias directs her thoughts. She notes that in the early stages of one's faith walk, it seems that God often "*takes the initiative*" and lets us "*simply follow on with Him.*" She likens it to the visible "*pillar of cloud*" by which God led the children of Israel through the desert. "*Then the obvious leading ceases. He is there, but He has withdrawn the pillar of cloud from before us, and asks us to go on in bare faith.*" He is still there, she observes, "*shielding and separating us in ways out of our ken, from the dangers that are seen by Him alone.*"

These are strong words, reassuring and comforting, from a veteran of faith in the final year of her life. I think of a conversation with yet another "veteran of faith" during her time of wrenching grief following the death of her husband. "Many people testify to uniquely sensing the presence of God during their time of loss. I wish I could say that was my experience," she confessed. "There were times I cried out to God and never *felt* His presence. And yet my belief that He was there was the very bedrock of my survival. I couldn't have made it without that knowledge." Years later, she referred to that time of "bare faith" saying, "I reread my journal entries, recording that period of time, and God's fingerprints were all over the pages!"

C. S. Lewis, in the Narnia chronicle *The Horse and His Boy*, provides a wonderful insight into God's loving care. This story relates the adventures of Bree, a talking horse and his boy, Shasta, as they embark on a mission to save Narnia from enemy invasion. Throughout their perilous journey, they are plagued by encounters with lions. During a dangerous night journey over a steep mountain pass, Shasta discovers he is accompanied by yet another lion. This time the lion speaks, revealing that the many lions Shasta has feared were actually one.

> I was the lion who forced you to join with Aravis. I was the cat who comforted you among the houses of the dead. I was the lion who drove the jackals from you while you slept. I was the lion who gave the Horses the new strength of fear for the last mile so that you should reach King Lune in time. And I was the lion you do not remember who pushed the boat in which you lay, a child near death, so that it came to shore where a man sat, wakeful at midnight, to receive you.

Aslan, the Christ-figure, had accompanied Shasta throughout his mission, becoming whatever Shasta needed to get safely home. "*Shielding and separating . . . in ways out of our ken, from the dangers that are seen by Him alone.*"

I want signs and wonders—clouds and fire—demonstrable proof that God is there . . . that He is hearing . . . leading. But sometimes, it seems, I am asked to go on in bare faith.

Why? I wonder. Is God testing me? Is He moving me forward in my journey of faith? (I'd rather stay in the relative safety of the wilderness with the reassuring cloud by day, fire by night.)

Who can know the mind of God in all the particulars of one's personal faith journey? We do know, however, that He promises: "Never will I leave you; never will I forsake you. Surely I am with you always, to the very end of the age (Hebrews 13:5; Matthew 28:20)." We may not see Him or recognize Him if we do. Yet all the while, He is there, being whatever it is—in ways "*out of our ken*"—that He knows we need for each moment.

So we journey on. Sometimes God takes the initiative and lets us follow on with Him. Sometimes the obvious leading stops—and we go on in bare faith. But all the while, He is there (yes!) "*shielding and separating us . . . from the dangers that are seen by Him alone.*"

Yes! He is there. He is *here*.

God, You promise that You are present even when I don't sense Your Presence. May I proceed in bare faith, believing that You are shielding and guiding me in ways I don't even perceive.

Parable of the Well Water

Such a lovely "beholding" today! I went to the well—and it was uncovered for me to look down. Instead of the still circle of water I expected to see, it was all heaving and rippling in swelling circles! Then it stopped and grew quiet, and while I was wondering if my eyes could have deceived me, the trembling began and all was repeated. Some periodic up-burst from the hidden spring below—then all grew glassy again. I never knew before what the "well of water springing up" meant. I thought of it vaguely as a springing all the time. But this is so much more like His way with our souls. A sudden rising and flooding of the underlying life—and then a sinking back with stillness.

—Diary June 15, 1909

"A fruitful bough by a well, whose branches run over the wall"

Painting: from Diary 1909

All my springs are in thee. —Psalm 87:7 KJV

THE IMMEDIATE CONTEXT for this parable of the well water was, in fact, a parable of faith. The site of a native mission house in the village of Blida was decided by the location of a potential well as determined by a water diviner. Having dug to a depth of fifty meters without striking water, the so-called expert suggested that water course had been diverted by earthquake activity. The local people read more into this: if God is pleased with you, why doesn't He give you water? Lilias was convinced that this was a test of faith and that they should proceed as planned. Weeks passed without reaching water, and the diggers, at last, abandoned the site.

The very next day, Lilias received a telegram reporting that the first trickle of water had begun, gradually filling the well! Later Lilias visited Blida and the mouth of the well was uncovered, allowing her to see down the shaft. She was initially startled by her observation of water "*heaving and rippling in swelling circles*" followed by a quieting to a "*still circle of water.*" She watched as a pattern emerged: "*Some periodic up-burst from the hidden spring below—then all grew glassy again.*"

This natural phenomena evoked a spiritual parallel: Like the water, God's presence is present, but one's experience of the same is in continual flux, sometimes "*heaving and rippling,*" sometimes "*a still circle.*"

The water in the well gave a picture of a reality that Lilias experienced over and over in her walk of faith. But perhaps never so poignantly as in the fall of 1897. Lilias was returning to Algiers from England, after a period of prolonged drought of the soul. With "storm clouds" gathering over their work in a worsening political climate for all things English, she felt as if she prayed to "*skies of brass.*" Then, on the train south through France, while reading her Bible, she received what she believed to be a promise from God: "The Lord, whom ye seek, shall suddenly come to his temple" (Malachi 3:1 KJV).

What follows is limited by this brief account, but she records "*such an unbelievable sense of light and sweetness and of the thirst of all those days being quenched in Himself.*" Her experience translated into a similar "blessing" not only for those who worked alongside her in Algiers but for many along the coast of North Africa who came by invitation for "four days with God." Hearts were softened and changed, relationships healed and restored: "*. . . heaving and rippling in swelling circles.*" People returned to their respective locations with hearts bursting with joy and spirits anticipating the next thing.

None more than Lilias, however. In her first diary entry of 1898, she wrote, "*The New Year is dawning full of hope and wondering for what it holds in store.*" Three months later came the poignant entry, "*Has that wave of blessing lost its impetus? Sometimes I feel that it has . . . There is blessing still, but looking round one feels that something has gone.*" "*. . . a sinking back with stillness.*"

She examined her soul for some grievance of her own that might have blocked the blessing, but she concluded, "*I am coming to see that our own 'experience'* [still vs. active waters] *so far, as a conscious emotional thing matters nothing, if He is free in His working all round.*"

Lilias's summing up of the varying experiences of faith speaks straight to my heart. I must admit that I am an experience-seeking pilgrim. I yearn, even barter, for the rippling waters to verify and validate my faith. My reality, in contrast, has been that there is not a thing I can do to induce a display of divine waterworks. I console myself: If Lilias with her mature spirituality couldn't curry favor with God, manifest in sustained emotion, then there is little hope that *my* pleading and praying would be the determinate factor! Furthermore, my bubbly water experiences are not only few and far between but, if I'm completely honest, utterly without circumstantial merit or predictable pattern. Often they come when I have least expected it—neither seeking nor deserving.

What, then, do I conclude about God's "*way with our souls*"? The source of water is constant, regardless of one's experience of the same. God is the source of the deep hidden spring, satisfying the parched hearts of those who drink from the living water. Little does it matter how I experience that water as long as I drink freely from the well that never runs dry.

There may be those memorable occasions when the waters heave and ripple in swelling circles. Grace. To which the appropriate response is "thank you" not "why not more often?" God knows when and where and why we might need the "*periodic up-burst from the hidden spring below.*" In the meanwhile, we trust Him for our experience of faith as well as the reality of His Presence. At the end of the day, it is not how I (or, for that matter, anyone else) perceives the water. It is simply receiving the life-giving, thirst-quenching waters of Him who said: "Whoever drinks the water I give him will never thirst. Indeed, the water I give him will become in him a spring of water welling up to eternal life" (John 4:14).

God, You are the constant source of living water. Let me not place my trust in fleeting emotions, but in the Well that will not run dry.

Sails to the Wind

I am seeing more and more that we begin to learn what it is to walk by faith when we learn to spread out all that is against us: all our physical weakness, loss of mental power, spiritual inability—all that is against us inwardly and outwardly—as sails to the wind and expect them to be vehicles for the power of Christ to rest upon us. It is so simple and self-evident—but so long in the learning!   —Diary August 22, 1902

Drawing: from 1877 Pocket Sketchbook: France/Switzerland/Venice

Likewise the Spirit also helps in our weakness. —Romans 8:26 NKJV

Small vessel, large body of water. Clear sea, blue skies, and a mountain view. Sailing is smooth in calm weather, but all that is needed to put that fragile craft at risk is a gust of wind from a sudden squall.

Small vessel, large body of water—a perfect picture of my vulnerability to the storms that assail me outwardly or inwardly. "*Physical weakness, loss of mental powers spiritual inability.*" Any of these could be enough to capsize the craft of my fragile self. More often it is all the above that conspire to my collapse, each swell or wave converging in force: my physical state affecting my mental and emotional state, taking its toll on my spiritual well-being.

Yet within this very picture of vulnerability is the solution for survival. My knee-jerk response to the waves that buffet me is varied: recoil, resist, fight back, cave in. The antidote that Lilias presents is straight from Scripture: take *all* that is against us—inner and outer—and hold them up as "sails" for God to empower. His "power is made perfect in weakness" (2 Corinthians 12:9). An exchange: my weakness for God's power.

What is "against" me? At start, I have certain physical limitations that invariably take a toll on other areas of my life—my state of mind, my emotions. And there are the outward forces which, like those summer squalls, come unexpectedly, often defeating me, if not in body, in soul. I must take all that is against me—inwardly and outwardly—and spread my weaknesses as sails for God's power.

What might this look like for someone else? The particulars will be individual: *physical weakness* (sleeplessness from night shifts with an infant, chronic pain, a permanent disability)—sails for God's power; *loss of mental powers* (relentless work pressures, pressing demands with studies, financial stress, depression)—sails for God's power; *spiritual inability* (character deficiencies, addictions, doubt, moral temptation even failure)—sails for God's power.

Storms beyond our control assail us throughout life. We pray the plight of the Breton fisherman: "Lord, Your sea is so vast, and my little boat is small."

God answers: "My grace is sufficient for you, for my power is made perfect in weakness" (2 Corinthians 12:9).

Lord, Your power is made perfect in weakness. Take my weakness and uncertainties and use them as vehicles for Your power.

Let Faith Swing Out on Him

"The things that are impossible with men are possible with God." Yes, face it out to the end. Cast away every shadow of hope on the human side as a positive hindrance to the Divine; heap the difficulties together recklessly, and pile on as many more as you can find: you cannot get beyond that blessed climax of impossibility. Let faith swing out on Him. He is the God of the impossible.   —*The Glory of the Impossible*

Painting: from Travel Journal 1896–1897

For nothing is impossible with God.   —Luke 1:37

AN EARLY MORNING, more than three decades ago, I awakened my husband with a strange request. Would it be all right with him if I went to the corner coffee shop to work something out in my mind? "I will be back in time to fix breakfast." He muttered something through his sleep that I interpreted as yes. On the way out the door, I grabbed a book from the bookshelf to give me an appearance of legitimacy. ("What is she doing here this time of morning, for goodness' sake?!")

Fact is, I had been wrestling for several months with a passion to write out my life with young children: a processing of the joys and challenges of the transition from being my mother's daughter to being my children's mother. I would find myself jotting down ideas on scraps of paper throughout the day or recording conversations or questions in my journal to "take up for further thought." Was I going crazy, or was there a point and purpose to my madness?

My plan was to have this out with myself and with God, once and for all. It seemed that I was scheming more than writing an article. Each new thought spawned a subthought or invited counterbalance. Development. Could it be a book? *Impossible.*

Impossible. I was the mother of three young children: a toddler, a preschooler, and an early grade schooler. Furthermore, my husband was a minister and his role invariably added additional responsibilities and time commitments to my life. When would I ever have any time to write a book-length manuscript? If I did, who would publish it? (No one was saying, "You ought to write a book, Miriam.") Moreover, who would read it?!

I ordered a mug of coffee and opened the book, *Adventures in Prayer* by Catherine Marshall, then leafed through the chapter titles. One caught my eye: "Prayer Helps Dreams Come True." I scanned the chapter, rich with real-life illustrations, which she concluded with a series of questions to help readers determine if a "dream" had sprung from selfish human will or the will of God. She had my full attention:

1. Will my dream fulfill the talents, the temperament, and emotional needs which God has planted in my being?

2. Does my dream involve taking anything or any person belonging to someone else?

3. Am I willing to make all my relationships with other people right?

4. Do I want this dream with my whole heart?

5. Am I willing to wait patiently for God's timing?

6. Am I dreaming big?

Am I dreaming big? I could literally feel chills pass through me as I read the final test. She elaborated: "The bigger the dream and the more persons it will benefit, the more apt it is to stem from the infinite designs of God."

Yes, this was big. *Impossible.* As I reviewed each of the six tests in light of my situation, I felt I had to present my reality to God. I didn't know how I could possibly write a book amid all my other responsibilities, but I was willing (a) to be faithful to those commitments; (b) if there was time left over, to use it to write. I did remind God that if this was truly His will for me, He would have to help me at each step of the way.

And He did. Every morning from that time on, I awakened at 5:30 without the aid of an alarm and wrote from six to seven at the corner coffee shop. I returned home in time to prepare breakfast and the children for their day. The rest of the writing, typing, and editing took place in small chinks of time throughout the day. Within a year, the book was written and accepted by Doubleday for publication. (How did that happen?) Five books later, I can honestly say that no other has been as easy, either in the writing or the publication, as that first book, titled *Keep These Things, Ponder Them in Your Heart.*

Amy Carmichael wrote in *Whispers of His Power*, "Our Lord is always asking the impossible of us. He is always trusting us to rise to it. And best of all, He is always standing alongside to make the impossible possible."

While this was perhaps the most dramatic working out of a dream—an impossibility—in my life, I've seen a pattern ever since for myself and for others: those things that God "asks" of us, some seemingly insignificant, some overwhelmingly immense, He also provides the strength and the insight and the determination to carry it to the finish.

This does not mean that there are not obstacles along the way or even delays in the results. Furthermore, the "end" might be quite different from the initial idea. (Some ideas are discarded along the way!) But for those things that *God* intends for our collaboration with His purposes, there are no difficulties, no hindrances that *"cannot get beyond that blessed climax of impossibility."*

"Let faith swing out on Him. He is the God of the impossible."

God, I see difficulties; You see possibilities.
Let my faith swing out to You, God of the impossible!

A Few Yards Further

. . . today's "first lesson" was in these little mountain paths. I followed mine only a few yards further this morning & such an outburst of beauty came. You can never tell to what untold glories any little humble path may lead, if you only follow far enough. —Diary August 13, 1899

Painting: from Journal 1899

You have made known to me the path of life;
    you will fill me with joy in your presence,
    with eternal pleasures at your right hand.   —Psalm 16:11

SWITZERLAND. Lilias takes a much-needed break from the work and weather of an Algerian summer. The cool mountain air provides a welcome contrast to the heat and humidity of the crowded Casbah.

She begins her day with a walk along a mountain pathway. The path itself is stony and rugged, the guiding fence in disrepair. The excursion promises no particular enticements but fresh air and a distant mountain view. But then, advance a few yards, and she is greeted by an unexpected burst of beauty!

Who has not had the experience of rounding a bend, on foot or in vehicle, to an unexpected vista: an open field of vibrant red poppies, the sudden dip to a lush green valley, a glimpse of lake shimmering in the sun. One can only wonder what "*untold glories*" we might have missed by stopping short.

The same can be experienced in the unseen world of the spirit. There are countless reasons for "stopping short" on the humble paths of the daily life: Discouragement: not much action on such an ordinary path. Fear: one never knows what dangers lurk in the unknown. Distraction: many are the enticements that lure one off course. Weariness: hardly enough energy to take another step. Lethargy: who cares, why even bother? Yet who knows what "untold glories" one might miss by not proceeding a bit further along the humble path.

The greatest blessings can come when we least expect them and in the most unexpected places. Most often it is when we are following the simple path set before us: the daily duty, the menial task. It comes along the humble path of daily obedience, if we "only follow far enough." In *My Utmost for His Highest* (March 29), Oswald Chambers says, "The only way a worker can remain true to God is to be ready for the Lord's surprise visits . . . This sense of expectation will give our life the attitude of childlike wonder He wants it to have."

My personal application of the mountain lesson is to intentionally cultivate a childlike sense of expectation—to be open to the possibility of the "*untold glories*" to which any little humble path may lead, if only I follow far enough.

❧ ❧ ❧

Lord, keep me free and expectant to the glorious possibilities that lie further down the path.

ACKNOWLEDGMENTS

A HEARTFELT THANK YOU to Larry and Anita Maxwell for making possible the devotional edition of *Images of Faith*. This complete edition—Volumes 1 & 2—would not be possible without their generosity and support. Their vision and valuing of Lilias's legacy likewise made possible the compilation of her art used in *A Blossom in the Desert* and its preservation for the future through their underwriting of high-quality digital images.

I will ever be grateful for the women who, influenced by the life, art, and writings of Lilias, have come alongside the vision to preserve her legacy and to present it to a new generation. My deepest gratitude to The Lilias Trotter Legacy Group: Darlene Kirk Hansen, Carol Holquist, Marjorie Lamp Mead, Sally Oxley, and Bonnie Camp Palmquist. Each woman has contributed liberally from her experience and expertise. Thank you!

A special word of appreciation to Evelyn Bence, consummate editor who, with her practical editorial skills, worked her alchemy on this manuscript and created a better book. My first editor for my first book forty years ago, Evelyn has remained throughout the years a true guide for and champion of my writing, a critic in the best sense of the word, an encourager—and friend. Thank you, Evelyn!

Thank you to Peter Gross, who so beautifully formatted *Images of Faith*, with all its design complexities, into this lovely devotional volume.

I can't begin to adequately express my gratitude to my husband, Dave, who has faithfully supported my research and writing from the beginning. His belief in me and in the value of Lilias sustained me throughout my entire journey with Lilias. There is no way to recount his tireless efforts and countless services on behalf of my passion to share Lilias with others. Without him, my story of Lilias would not have been told.

ABOUT THE AUTHOR

As author of *A Passion for the Impossible*, Miriam Huffman Rockness is the principal biographer of Lilias Trotter—a student of John Ruskin who gave up a promising art career to spread God's love with the people of Algeria. Miriam was the driving force behind *A Blossom in the Desert*, a compilation of Trotter's inspirational art and writings. Her narrative voice flows throughout the documentary film about Lilias, *Many Beautiful Things*. Miriam's personal reflections can be found through liliastrotter.com or directly at ililiastrotter.wordpress.com/.